Group Rhythm and Drumming with Older Adults: Music Therapy Techniques and Multimedia Training Guide

Barbara Reuer, PhD, NMT, MT-BC
Barbara Crowe, MM, MT-BC
Barry Bernstein, MT-BC

D1410786

AMERICAN
MUSIC
THERAPY
ASSOCIATION

ISBN:	1-884914-17-9
Authors:	Barbara Reuer, PhD, NMT, MT-BC
	Barbara Crowe, MM, MT-BC
	Barry Bernstein, MT-BC
Copyright Information:	©American Music Therapy Association, Inc. 2007
	8455 Colesville Road, Suite 1000
	Silver Spring, MD 20910 USA
	www.musictherapy.org
	info@musictherapy.org

Editorial Assistance:	Barbara Else, AMTA Consultant
Design and Layout:	Tawna Grasty, Grass T Design

Printed in the United States of America

Thank you to Remo, Inc. and West Music Company, Inc. for their generous contributions in support of this publication. Their continued promotion of music therapy and music making throughout our communities is most appreciated!

Remo, Inc

West Music Company, Inc

Special thanks to Dr. Andrea Farbman, AMTA Executive Director, Barbara Else, AMTA Consultant, and Tawna Grasty, Graphic Designer, for their guidance.

We would like to acknowledge the following for their assistance in the production of the DVD:

Elliott Lum, Deja View Digital Productions

DVD rhythym exercise participants:
Joy Givers (Volunteers)/
Diane Beckman, Jan Bluemer, Jill Hacker, Ann Hein, Jerry and Linda Lysne, Amber Rieder, Barbara Zurawski
Music Therapists/
Mutsumi Abiru (Japan), Anna Cafazza (Virginia), Destiny Fonville (California), Paula Heidman-Best (California), Cynthia Tate (North Carolina), Ally Yoon (Korea)

This manual is an outgrowth of a project, supported, in part, by grant number 90AT0541, 1993-1994, from the Administration on Aging, Department of Health and Human Services, Washington, DC 20201. The project co-investigators were E. Percil Stanford, PhD formally of the University Center on Aging as San Diego State University and Barbara Reuer, PhD, NMT, MT-BC.

◎◎ CONTENTS ◎◎

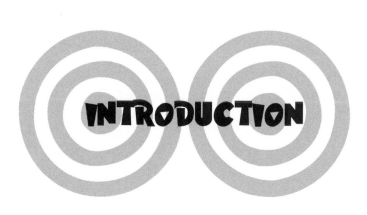

This best practice multimedia training guide utilizing group percussion strategies for promoting volunteerism with older adults is intended for use by music therapists, music educators, musicians, recreational therapists, activity directors, volunteer coordinators and others who would like to learn how to apply some of the approaches and techniques used in music therapy to work with well older adults. The training guide will prepare leaders to train volunteers as recreational group leaders using a specific group percussion/rhythm curriculum. Supporting literature confirms the belief that training older adults to volunteer in specific ways increases their motivation to become volunteers and the likelihood of their ongoing commitment to the volunteer program (Raynor, 2007; Zedlewski, S. & Schaner, S., 2006).

A DEMOGRAPHIC REVOLUTION

The United States and the entire world are currently experiencing a demographic revolution. In a little over 200 years, life expectancy in the United States has doubled, and according to the National Center for Health Statistics, life expectancy continues to rise (NCHS, 2005). For the first time in history, a society of healthy, active older adults has emerged. Throughout recorded history only one-in-ten people could expect to live to the age of 65. Today nearly 80% of all Americans will live past that age. Experts claim that by the year 2050, the average life expectancy of men and women in the U.S. could reach 89, up from 76 in 1995 (Peyser, 1999). This increase leads to a dramatic rise in the oldest segment of our population; Americans 85 and older are the *"There* fastest growing segment of the U.S. population *have been* (American Medical Student Association, *baby booms* 2005). In 1996, there were almost 4 *before, but* million people in the U.S. over 85 years *never a senior* old. By the year 2040, 13 million Ameri-*boom"* cans will be older than 85 (Alliance for Aging Research, 1996), an increase of more than thirty fold (U.S. Census Bureau, 2002). Until recently, work dominated the waking hours and most people worked right up until they died. That has changed. There have been baby booms before, but never a senior boom (Dychtwald & Fowler, 1990). The over-65 population in the United States will soon number 40-45 million representing one-fifth of the population. The older adult population will increase dramatically (both in numbers and as a percentage) during the first part of the 21st century.

MUSIC THERAPY PRACTICE

Music therapy practice with infirmed or frail elderly people in nursing homes and adult daycare settings is extensive and well documented (Prickett, 2000). A variety of music therapy activity interventions including group singing, reminiscing activities and movement to music are used to remediate a variety of problem areas (Davis, Gfeller, & Thaut, 1999). Recent research has shown that music therapy activity interventions are effective in promoting improved walking gait in stroke patients, improved movement and speech in patients with Parkinson's disease (Thaut, et al., 2001), decreased depression (Suzuki, 1998), improved social and interpersonal interactions (Clair, 2002), and improved cognitive functioning of persons with Alzheimer's disease (Holmes, Knights, Dean, et al.; Suzuki, et al., 2004). Music therapists are well aware of the benefits of music therapy interventions with infirmed elderly clients. Recent studies are supporting the need for more evidence-based protocols for recreation music-making as a means of inspiring creativity and wellness amongst older adults (2006; Bittman, Berk, Shaman, et al., 2005; Bittman, Bruhn, Lim, et al., 2004).

THE WELLNESS MOVEMENT

Living a healthy, active life style has become of major importance to all Americans. More and more of us are concerned about physical fitness. Wellness and enrichment of life are the objectives of many Americans. This is especially true of older people.

The customary ways of dealing with the aged population in the United States (institutional housing and costly, reactive medical interventions) will no longer be viable because of the enormous costs and the changing needs of a much larger and more active senior population. Several needs arise from this situation including:

1. Specific training and models of involvement and volunteerism that encourage and promote useful contributions to society for active well older Americans; and
2. The need for community-based programs and opportunities to promote communication between generations and prepare citizens for the aging process.

Music therapy was recognized as one possible means to address the needs outlined above as a result of the Special Hearing before the United Senate Special Committee on Aging (1991) and the subsequent amendments to the Older Americans Act of 1992.

The potential for the use of music therapy strategies with the well older adult is great. As Dr. Alicia Clair noted in her testimony before the Senate Special Committee on Aging, active music programs with well older adults can be innovative and preventative, stressing quality of life through active participation, physical and mental activity and socialization (U.S. Special Committee on Aging, 1991, p. 50). Since older adults can learn new musical skills very late in life (Clair, 1996) and music remains motivating and enjoyable throughout our lives, using music therapy approaches for work with well older adults is a natural expansion of music therapy practice. Because the population of individuals over age 65 is increasing rapidly in this country, work with well older adults is a growing and potentially large market for music therapy services.

> *"The potential for the use of music therapy strategies with the well older adult is great."*

The purpose of this training guide is to prepare leaders to work with well older adults in programs designed to train and empower these well seniors to conduct volunteer rhythm/drumming groups with peers in their communities. Though older adults could volunteer with any age group, for the purposes of the first phase of this program, a decision was made to focus on encouraging volunteer work with older adult peer groups. It was felt that senior volunteers could relate easily to their peers, would provide positive role models, would foster positive peer identification, and would, therefore, more readily and easily make a contribution to their communities. The following objectives have been set for these training materials:

13

- To provide professional leaders information on successfully working with and training well older adults to function as volunteer group leaders,

- To introduce leaders to the techniques and basic skills inherent in this percussion/ rhythm curriculum,

- To provide leaders with a complete 4-week training program and all necessary materials to work with older adult volunteers,

- To provide information on expanding music therapy practice into the area of health promotion and prevention,

- To train leaders to conduct successful presentations, and

- To provide information on financing, developing and marketing group programs.

RHYTHM-BASED MUSIC THERAPY

The group percussion/rhythm curriculum introduced in this training guide is derived from the principles and approaches developed from music therapy practice with infirmed older persons. This rhythm-based music therapy (RBMT) is a music therapy technique based on clients' active participation in a series of carefully selected and planned percussion/drumming activities. This technique uses instruments, rhythmic patterns and techniques from a number of ethnic traditions from around the world and emphasizes a cooperative, group-oriented model of participation. RBMT techniques were selected as a basis for this program to train volunteers to conduct recreational and diverse group percussion activities for the following reasons:

- ◎ Response to rhythm is basic to human functioning making these RBMT percussion activities and techniques highly motivating;
- ◎ Pure percussion activities are interesting and enjoyable to all people regardless of ethnic and cultural background, musical preferences or age making these activities useful for creating groups that are fun and positive for a wide variety of people;
- ◎ Participation in active group percussion experiences has physical benefits including sustained physical activity and use of fine motor skills;

◎ A strong sense of group identity and a feeling of belonging is created because: (a) participants are actively making music together; and (b) the sustained repetition of the steady beat acts to bring people together physically, emotionally and mentally (a process known as rhythmic entrainment);

◎ Percussion activities can be done with little or no previous musical background or training making these experiences accessible to people of all socioeconomic levels thus making it easy for senior volunteers to learn and teach others; and

◎ These techniques use multi-ethnic instruments and activities, which are increasingly important in our multi-ethnic and diverse society.

It is not the intention of this program to train volunteers to conduct music therapy sessions but rather to use activities and strategies adapted from music therapy practice to provide techniques for these volunteers to function as recreational music group leaders and activity assistants to professional music therapists.

SUMMARY

15

It is hoped that this training guide will prepare leaders to develop, set up, finance, market and conduct a series of classes for older adults designed to train volunteers as group percussion leaders. The training guide will first present information on working with the well older adult. Specific approaches and strategies for maximizing participation, motivation and learning for this group will be discussed. Then the specific group percussion/rhythm curriculum designed to train volunteers in group percussion activities will be outlined. Goals and objectives for such groups will be delineated, group facilitation principles outlined and the entire training experience including topics to cover, activities and instrument needs will be included. The training guide will also include information for leaders on how to develop materials and handouts, fund and market the volunteer training classes, network with aging organizations, and make a successful presentation.

"Involvement in the rhythmic aspects of music is basic and primal."

Though music therapy practices utilize a wide variety of music activities, group percussion strategies were chosen because research indicates great potential for the use of these activities with older adults, and because rhythm is the basis of all music, and in fact, all life (U.S. Special committee on Aging, 1991; Clair, 1996). Involvement in the rhythmic aspects of music is basic and primal. Research indicated that group percussion/rhythm experiences for older adults have the potential to offer a number of benefits such as immediate reduction of feelings of loneliness and improved nonverbal communications (Clair, 1996). The natural results are increased self-esteem, and enhanced ability to focus the mind, and group percussion/ rhythm experiences are just plain fun (Bittman, Bruhn, Lim, et al., 2004).

All training programs and activities established because of the use of this multimedia training guide are the responsibility of the individuals and/or the facility, institution or organization. It is our experience that the sponsoring facility, institution or organization typically carries liability insurance to cover professionals and volunteers. You, as a volunteer trainer, may want to ask sponsoring administrators what their policy is regarding liability for professionals and volunteers in case of injury.

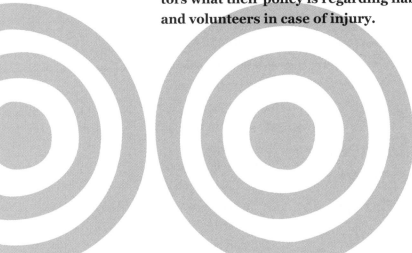

WORKING WITH OLDER ADULTS

It is well documented that the population of the United States is aging and growing because of increased life spans through improved medical intervention, preventive health practices, improved nutrition, and the swell of the baby boomer generation entering their 60s in the next 10-15 years. It is estimated that by the year 2010, 25% of the population will be over age 55, 6.8 million of them over the age of 85. Though this group of older adults is more active and healthier than ever before, they are still affected by the decrements of motor, sensory and mental functioning that occur as we age, as well as the social and economic changes common to older persons.

To date, music therapy practice has focused primarily on the small percentage of older persons who are considered infirmed or senescent: those individuals who have serious impairment in physical, cognitive, sensory and social functioning due to disease, including Alzheimer's disease, stroke, Organic Brain Syndrome and major mental health problems. This practice is well established and emphasizes remediation of serious functioning loss. In order for music therapy professionals to successfully move into work with the well older adult, two things must occur: (1) the focus of our work must shift to supportive activities emphasizing health maintenance, habilitation, and wellness; and, (2) the therapist must understand the changes in physical functioning, learning styles, motivation and social responses that occur naturally as we age. This section of the training guide will supply you with information on the older adult learner to enable you to successfully work with well older adults.

"It is estimated that by the year 2010, 25% of the population will be over age 55..."

The information contained in this chapter is for the use of leaders and volunteers. It is not intended for direct dissemination to the general participants. When teaching some of this background material during training workshops, be aware that the older adult may be sensitive to this information about changes in their functioning and plan your presentation accordingly.

MYTHS AND FACTS ABOUT AGING

One of the best ways to determine our own assumptions about aging and older people is to examine myths of aging. Many of these myths are usually over-generalizations that portray all older adults as infirmed. Read these myths located on the next page to see if you have false assumptions about "old people."

MYTHS vs. FACTS

Myth: *All old people are the same.*
Fact: As a group, older adults are more heterogeneous than any other. They have had greater opportunities to develop individual differences, interests and opinions. Individual personality traits and coping mechanisms, not aging per se, determine peoples' behavior and opinions later in life.

Myth: *Senility and mental decline are inevitable parts of the aging process.*
Fact: Senility is not a natural part of the aging process. Old age does not mean inevitable decline in memory and cognitive acuity. In fact, only 20-25% of older adults ever develop organic brain disorders, and most of those are aged 85+.

Myth: *Self-esteem and feelings of self-worth decrease as we age.*
Fact: In general, older people have a positive sense of self and an overall high level of life satisfaction. However, severe losses in physical functioning and social status, impaired communication and isolation can impact on self-image.

Myth: *Intelligence declines with age.*
Fact: Intellectual functioning does not decline for older individuals; many even improve as they age, especially if they stay mentally active and challenged. The older adult years are frequently a time of increased creativity and intellectual productivity.

Myth: *Old age is a time of blissful rest and reflection. Old people do not have a care in the world.*
Fact: Old age can be a time of stress, uncertainty and loss. The elderly can suffer from mental health problems such as loss-related depression (up to 25% of older people). Depression is often referred to as the common cold of old age and is frequently misdiagnosed as Organic Brain Syndrome. However, depression is treatable and its impact on functioning may be minimized.

Myth: *Old people are unproductive and have little to offer.*
Fact: Older people remain active and concerned about their personal and community relations (Clair, 1996). Older adults want to share their knowledge and experience and have a need to leave a legacy to subsequent generations.

Myth: *Most older people move to sunny, warm climates after retirement.*
Fact: Most retirees remain in the same location they spent their adult lives near family and friends. The needs of the well older person must be addressed in every community across the country and not in a few Sunbelt "retirement" areas.

Myth: *All older people live out their later years in nursing facilities.*
Fact: Only about one percent of the older population lives in institutional settings of this one percent, 75% do not have a spouse or other form of community support and most have serious medical problems. Lack of family or community support of older people is the most critical factor in forcing institutionalization settings (U.S. Census Bureau, 2001; GenAmerica, 2001).

FUNCTIONING OF OLDER ADULTS

We will look at three areas of functioning of older adults—**PHYSICAL FUNCTIONING** including motor behavior, cognitive skills and sensory changes, **PSYCHOLOGICAL EMOTIONAL FUNCTIONING** and mental health issues, and **SOCIAL FUNCTIONING** and need for group and peer affiliation.

PHYSICAL FUNCTIONING

The natural physical changes that occur as we age have four characteristics:

1. These changes are universal. Everyone is affected, but what constitutes those effects is different for each person. Individual change depends on genetics, life situation, social/economic factors, ability to adjust to change and general health. All events in life affect how a person ages and causes each person to age uniquely (Davis, Gfeller, & Thaut, 1999).

2. The onset of change is gradual and accommodation to these changes occurs without conscious awareness over a period of many years. This diminishes the psychological impact of the diminishing of functioning.

3. Though not debilitating until very late in life, physical changes associated with aging are progressive and detrimental. Changes in behavior such as diet and exercise patterns may slow the progress of change but, over time, diminishing of functioning will occur.

4. Normal age related changes are intrinsic to the individual occurring regardless of outside events. Environmental factors may only hasten or slow the progress of change. It is important for those working with older adults to recognize that changes in many areas of functioning will occur and to make necessary accommodations so that the older individual can maintain active, meaningful involvement in activities.

We will now look at the physical changes that naturally occur as we age. Each section will be in three parts—physiological changes, effects of these changes on functioning, and points to remember for accommodating for these changes when doing music groups with well older people.

MOTOR CHANGES

1. Decrease in the number of muscle fibers

2. Muscle cells replaced by fat cells

3. Decrease in elasticity of muscles

4. Thinner, more brittle bones

5. Some reduction in height

6. Changes in the central nervous system that impacts on motor behavior.

These physiological changes cause a general decrease in strength, stamina, flexibility and reaction time. Older people fatigue more quickly after the onset of physical activity and have decreased efficiency of performance for complicated motor tasks.

POINTS TO REMEMBER

Motor Changes

1. Vigorous physical activity, such as drumming, needs to be carefully paced to avoid fatigue. Alternate drumming with singing, body percussion and hand percussion activities.

2. Rotate instruments used by group members to prevent muscle fatigue and problems with over-usage of isolated muscle groups.

3. Don't judge fatigue level based on your personal reactions but on what you observe in your group members.

NEURO-SENSORY CHANGES

1. Decrease in number of neurons in the central nervous system

2. Decrease in brain weight and volume

3. Increase in fat composition of neurons

4. Changes in the myelin sheath (covering of the neurons)

5. Slowing of alpha brain waves (associated with a relaxed, awake state)

Generally these changes decrease the speed at which the central nervous system processes and reacts to information and the ability of the body to cope with environmental stressors. Neuro-sensory changes during aging are widespread and influence a number of skills and behavior including motor response, memory, intelligence and ability to learn. The specific effects of these changes follow.

Intelligence—In normal aging, there is little change in intelligence especially if an individual is maintaining mental activity. Reduced ability for complex decision making, decrease in speed of thought and some forms of perception are affected by normal aging. However, there is little or no loss in verbal comprehension, social awareness and application of experience.

Memory—There are some slight changes in memory functioning as we age, but these changes can be countered by mental and physical activity, rehearsal time and changes in presentation of material. The older adult easily learns the compensation strategies for the benign senescent forgetfulness of aging. Research has shown that older persons do experience some problem in both acquiring new information and recall of that information once it has entered long-term memory though this is most prominent in the very old. Memory is affected more by changes in daily routine, general levels of fatigue, stress, depression, complexity of task to be remembered, speed of information presentation during learning and attempts to recall information not recently used. The older learner tends to remember information better when presented visually than they do the same information presented auditorially (Ciocon & Potter, 1988, p. 44).

Ability to Learn—Older people can learn new skills and information. However, there are changes in how older adults learn, the efficiency of encoding new information into long-term memory and their ability to do necessary memory work. The older adult learner does not spontaneously organize and categorize material, does not do adequate rehearsal of information, employs fewer mnemonic devices and often lacks the motivation necessary for learning to occur.

23

POINTS TO REMEMBER

Neuro-Sensory Changes

1. When teaching a new skill, include adequate rehearsal time into your activity presentation. For example, do not assume they "have it" after one or two repetitions of a song or rhythm pattern. Be sure that your efforts to rehearse new skills are very musical and highly motivating—no boring rhythm drills.

2. Use a number of visual cues to aid learning—visual charts of rhythm patterns, visual modeling of skills. Be particularly aware of this when doing call and response activities. Be sure they can see you do the desired rhythmic pattern as well as hear and rhythmically feel or internalize it.

3. When teaching new skills or tasks, present material in simple, non-complicated steps. Do a task analysis of activities and teach component skills separately. The more choices involved in a task, the longer it takes to learn, so keep choices limited.

4. Do not present material too quickly. Rushing through rhythm patterns or words to songs will make learning difficult and frustrating for the older adult.

5. Include memory work in your activities. Provide the mnemonics (words for rhythm patterns) and categorization (tell them how a new pattern relates to previously learned materials.)

6. Allow time for response, particularly a motor skill since reaction time slows.

7. Do motoric modeling of rhythm patterns when needed.

8. Older learners seem to be more successful when the discovery method is used where the older learner discovers for themselves the correct method of performing tasks under conditions in which they have little chance of making errors (Connor, 2002). The basic principle of music therapy, "structuring for success" is very applicable here.

SENSORY CHANGES

Auditory

1. Hearing sensitivity decreases.

2. Incidence of hearing impairment increases (Up to 60% of older persons have some degree of hearing loss).

3. Decreased sensitivity to loudness changes.

4. Loss of ability to hear very high and very low frequencies

5. Distortions of sounds particularly in the range of human speech and musical forms.

Generally, loss of auditory sensitivity has serious and far-reaching consequences to the older individual. Hearing loss causes impairment in the ability to communicate and may lead to increasing social isolation. The inability to hear or understand speech can create personality changes, add to depression, decrease ability to do reality testing and cause social paranoia. Physical activity, reaction time and general health can also be impacted negatively. Hearing loss can also contribute to the impression of loss of intelligence since a decrease in performance on verbal test of intellectual ability is noted.

Vision

1. Vision impairments are not as prevalent as once thought and most vision problems may be remedied or controlled with medications, correction with glasses, cataract removal with lens implantation, and environmental changes such as lighting adjustments, reduction of glare, and structural accommodations.

2. Structural changes occur in the eye including a decrease in muscle elasticity causing problems in focusing.

3. Certain diseases such as age-related macular degeneration affect central vision.

4. Decrease in amount of light entering the retina also affects vision.

Vision losses may cause some problems in mobility and general ability to cope with the environment. Participation in group activities dependent on visual cues may be affected.

Other Sensory Changes

Changes occur in all sensory channels. Of particular interest in music activities are changes in the vestibular system, which regulates balance, motor stability and general orientation. Changes in this sense can cause problems in balance and equilibrium and a general sense of being unstable on your feet.

POINTS TO REMEMBER

Sensory Changes

1. Provide high levels of non-glare light for group experiences especially when teaching new skills and techniques.

2. When using visual aids like rhythm charts use contrasting colors that maximize visibility (although use of color can vary by individual preference and the nature of visual impairment). Locate visuals at a height visible for persons with bi- and trifocal corrections.

3. Know who your visually impaired group members are and help them learn skills through auditory and motoric modeling.

4. Limit the amount of locomotor movement in activities to avoid falls from vestibular insecurity.

5. Be especially sensitive to hearing difficulties of group members since the majority of older adult learners will have some amount of hearing problems.

6. Speak clearly, slowly, and facing the group members. Do not shout since it only distorts your voice tone and facial expression.

7. Get group members attention before speaking or demonstrating a musical skill.

8. Lower the pitch of your voice to help facilitate understanding of speech.

9. Repeat instructions using different words.

10. Try to limit extraneous background noise including random playing of rhythm instruments.

11. Remember that older persons may be sensitive to loud sounds and react negatively to a high sound level. This is particularly true of individuals wearing hearing aids. Help them make the necessary adjustments to be comfortable in the activity.

12. Structure the environment for safety—keep equipment out of the way to avoid tripping, have firm chairs with straight backs, unclutter your room, avoid highly polished floors and scatter rugs.

13. Be aware that older persons do not adapt to environmental changes easily, especially temperature variations. Rooms may need to be warmer than is comfortable for you.

PSYCHOLOGICAL /EMOTIONAL FUNCTIONING

Old age is not a mental illness and aging normally does not create insurmountable psychological problems. Our older years, however, do present unique challenges to our psychological well-being, coping skills, levels and types of motivation, and interpersonal relationships. Just as in other stages of human development, old age, too, has its own characteristic developmental tasks—to clarify, deepen and find use for what one has already learned in life and to accept that one's life has been meaningful (Davis, Gfeller, & Thaut, 1999). Older individuals may have a need to leave a legacy, share knowledge and expertise with the community at large and maintain a sense of control over their lives. Aging in our society is characterized by a need to cope with a number of losses including loss of physical capacities, loss of social role through retirement and widowhood, loss of spouse and loved ones, loss of economic status, and loss from re-location. This may create a high level of psychological stress and can tax even the best coping skills.

MOTIVATION

Motivation to participate in an activity to learn new skills and knowledge is dependent on the older person's willingness to use their capacities to the fullest. The activity or new learning has to have enough meaning for them to participate. Several characteristic factors of motivation in older people exist.

1. Older individuals are often hesitant to commit themselves to action.
2. There is a tendency for them to be overly cautious and con cerned about "doing it right."
3. Skills achieved are valued more highly if the effort required to learn them has been relatively great (Welford, 1975).

Motivation

1. Be aware of the natural tendency for older learners to be cautious and hesitant about demonstrating a new skill until they feel it is correct. When giving instructions, be very concrete and use no extraneous words. Give instructions three or four times. Model the activity. Start with the most alert participants.

2. Plan your training program in such a way that the older adult knows that they have had to work and expend effort to learn these new skills.

3. You may need to provide motivation for learning to be a volunteer group percussion leader by sharing with the senior trainees why this activity is useful to them and other older adults. Such rationales may include the following:

- Developing interests or hobbies such as group percussion keeps the mind alert and the body active.
- Staying active and learning new skills is the best way for older people to remain sharp and keep their full mental abilities including memory.
- Group percussion is a natural group activity and is a fun way to socialize and combat loneliness.
- Making music together promotes a sense of belonging; volunteers are helping others while helping themselves at the same time.

COPING SKILLS

A person's ability to cope with the loss, change and stress of the aging process is dependent on lifelong personality traits and their personal pattern of reaction to change. To successfully age, individuals must have adequate coping skills to deal with their decrease in physical abilities, changes in life roles, loss of social group and possible economic changes. Unsuccessful coping strategies may lead to decreased feelings of self-worth, anger and an inability to experience pleasure. Stabilization and restoration of the individual's sense of self, increased interpersonal competence, and acquisition of cognitive and behavioral skills are coping skills and defense mechanisms that are common to older adults (Leszcz, 1997). Butler (1983) identifies a number of defense mechanisms and coping skills that are common to older people. These include projection (attributing our own feelings outward onto others), denial, intellectualization (viewing the world without emotion), repression (blocking out stressful memories or situations), and selective sensory reception.

MENTAL HEALTH

As previously noted, old age is not a mental illness. However, older individuals do experience anxiety, stress and, particularly, depression. Depression may be a bigger problem in the well older person than once was thought and may effect up to 50% of older individuals at some point in their lives (Clair, 1996). Unresolved grief for the losses associated with aging is the single largest contributor to depression in older people. This depression will be evidenced in older adults through slowed response and reaction times, social isolation, memory problems, decrease in self-worth, physical fatigue and generalized physical complaints, irritability, and impatience.

POINTS TO REMEMBER

Coping Skills and Mental Health

1. Support group members in experiencing and expressing emotions in appropriate ways. Give many examples so that participants are not uncomfortable. Use third-party examples, e.g., "My niece said . . ."

2. Be aware of defense mechanisms being used especially projection and over cautiousness to avoid frustration on your part.

3. Acknowledge participant's experience and expertise.

4. It is all right to have fun. This generation of older adults comes from a work ethic and sometimes feels guilty when having fun.

5. Focus on people's positive coping skills and abilities, emphasizing what they already know.

6. This generation of older adults, especially women, grew up in a society where they were expected to please. Rather than participate and do the activity incorrectly, they will choose not to respond or just smile.

SOCIAL FUNCTIONING

Older adults experience changes in interpersonal roles and ways of relating to others because of widowhood, retirement, separation from family members, and loss of support groups through re-location. Many older individuals are lonely because they live alone, have lost a sense of belonging and have increasingly isolated themselves. This is particularly true if they are experiencing hearing loss, depression or ill health. The older person often needs to work to maintain or re-establish patterns of communication, develop positive peer identification, establish social contacts, and create feelings of affiliation. Group participation and group work is important for the older adult for a number of reasons:

1. Participation in groups combats loneliness, isolation and withdrawal. Well established music therapy theory states that music is a natural,

non-threatening group experience and that active participation in group music making has the ability to form and maintain group experiences and a sense of belonging (Davis, Gfeller, & Thaut, 1999).

2. Interacting with other older adults helps develop positive peer identification through the discovery of shared commonalties and experiences.

3. Groups act as laboratories for learning new patterns of interaction, communication and social relations.

4. Group experiences are a support to self-esteem through new skill building and sharing skills and knowledge with other people. In group music, participants can be a leader, soloist, teacher or a valued "member of the band."

5. Group experiences are intrinsically fun, pleasurable and satisfying for older people. This is especially true of groups that are actively making music such as the percussion/rhythm groups outlined in this training guide.

POINTS TO REMEMBER

Social Functioning

1. Have a clear structure to the group percussion/rhythm sessions.

2. Encourage participants to talk during sessions about how to use and apply information and skills.

3. Deal with peer-to-peer disagreements, irritation and impatience.

4. Encourage peer-to-peer direct communication, skill, and knowledge sharing.

5. Reinforce volunteers that they are doing a good job. Encourage volunteers to be patient and not demanding of their peers. (Teach volunteers to avoid words such as: *"No, that is not right"* or *"No!"* Instead, try words such as *"You might want to try."*)

TRAINING CURRICULUM

This chapter contains the various components of the rhythm-based training curriculum:

A. RESPONSIBILITIES OF VOLUNTEERS;

B. GROUP PERCUSSION RHYTHM FACILITATION PRINCIPLES;

C. GOALS AND OBJECTIVES OF A PERCUSSION RHYTHM PROGRAM;

D. SAMPLE OF A FOUR-WEEK TRAINING CURRICULUM;

E. SUPERVISION SUGGESTIONS; AND

F. RHYTHM-BASED EXERCISES WARM-UP, GROUP FOCUS, AND RHYTHM DRUMMING .

RESPONSIBILITIES OF VOLUNTEERS

1. Have a thorough knowledge of your subject matter.

2. Have a desire and the teaching skills to communicate the information to others.

3. Have leadership qualities, tact, patience and a sense of humor.

4. Have organizational abilities to make teaching methods appropriate to the older adult learner, the situation and the subject matter.

5. Hold a belief that older adults continue to learn.

6. Respect your older adult learners.

7. Be a good "time-keeper" so sessions are well paced and all material is covered.

8. Respond empathetically and honestly.

9. Be responsive to the emotions, struggles and anxieties that your participants may be experiencing especially as you introduce this new behavior of "drumming" (Waters, Weaver, & White, 1980).

GROUP PERCUSSION/
RHYTHM FACILITATION PRINCIPLES

1. The chosen activities should meet individual and group needs.

- Rhythms chosen should be within the physical and cognitive capabilities of each individual.
- Each participant should be offered an instrument, which allows for individual choice and best meets his/her physical needs.

2. Resistive attitudes are best dealt with by offering each participant an instrument on an individual basis.

3. Whenever possible begin working in small groups.

- Groups of 4-6 are beneficial to introduce rhythm concepts.
- A group size of 10-12 allows participants to learn and experience layered rhythm playing without being over stimulated.

4. Use physical/vocal cuing to model rhythmic responses.

- Whenever possible try to have participants vocalize the rhythm pattern.
- Introduce new rhythms by modeling hand/arm movements with out drums.
- This can be done with arms out in front of body, as if playing a conga, or by playing knees like bongos.
- Whenever demonstrating new activities/rhythms, exaggerated physical cues can be effective.
- Whenever possible have participants move their bodies to the new rhythm.
- Tapping toe to pulse, walking in step, or walking in a circle all help to solidify the pulse.

5. The level of participation by the leader is determined by what the group needs to experience the activity to its fullest potential. Withdraw as an active facilitator as the group is able to function independently.

6. Encourage participants to visualize their mallet or hand bouncing off the drumhead rather than hitting it. This will help them play with a lighter touch.

7. **Ability to make eye contact with participants is a factor in considering facilitator's placement in the circle.**

   • Facilitator should be part of the circle in small groups, 1-20 persons.
   • Facilitator should be in the center of the circle in groups of 20 or more for most activities.

8. **Responses to an activity may vary from person to person.**

   • Facilitators' expectations must be flexible.

9. **Mallet playing is more conducive to participation than hand drumming. Because of skin thinning, older people bruise easily.**

GOALS AND OBJECTIVES OF PERCUSSION/RHYTHM PROGRAM

The percussion/rhythm sessions are divided into four components to offer all participants a wide variety of experiences and establish session boundaries. The average session should be approximately 45-50 minutes in length. The four basic components of each session are as follows:

1. Warm-Up (Sharing)

The first component serves as a means to bring the group together. It is very important to offer these types of "ice-breaker" activities to encourage and build a feeling of trust within the group. The goals are:

   • To encourage social interaction in a structured environment
   • To provide an alternative means of social interaction.
   • To provide opportunity for individual choice within the group.
   • To improve concentration.
   • To offer opportunity for reinforcing short-term memory.

2. Group Focus (Community and/or Team Building)

The second component consists of activities designed to help participants become focused while at the same time developing a greater awareness of the group. Many of these activities will be basic rhythm warm-up exercises or simple relaxation techniques, which encourage participants to feel a basic pulse with their whole body. The goals are:

- To provide participants with alternative strategies for dealing with stress.
- To improve attention span.
- To provide opportunity for increased body awareness.

3. Rhythm/Drumming Activities
(Working on Skill Development)

These activities will involve basic team building exercises combined with percussive skill development for the participants and some basic ethno-musicological education. The goals are:

- To encourage feelings of self-worth via the process of creating something meaningful.
- To encourage feelings of self-worth via the process of learning a new skill.
- To encourage participants to spontaneously interact with others.
- To encourage self-expression.
- To maintain visual/motor skills and prevent deterioration of muscle tone.
- To provide opportunity for individual choice within the group.
- To provide opportunity for participants to work cooperatively with others.
- To improve concentration and increase attention span.
- To offer opportunity for reinforcing short/long-term memory.
- To develop interest in music as a redirection of leisure time.
- To learn (relearn) to enjoy music and movement simply for its own inherent qualities.
- To have fun.

4. Closure

The final section serves as a means for the group leader to say good-bye to the participants and helps to frame the group experience by ending with a structured activity.

4-WEEK TRAINING CURRICULUM

The following is provided as a model, only. (You, as the trainer of volunteers, might decide to do a 6-week or 8-week program.) The following 4-week training curriculum contains week-by-week outline of the four activity components and the suggested activities. The train-

38

ing classes are scheduled in 3-hour blocks. In addition to the weekly curriculum, a brief explanation of supervision is included. It is implied that all the activities and the method in which they are conducted shall be flexible and will be adapted to best meet the specific needs of your group.

It is strongly encouraged that during this training program that the trainer and the volunteer trainees follow the components of curriculum closely. We have found that if volunteers feel confident with these activities, they will have successful experiences in leading various groups and contributing to program reliability and sustainability.

WEEK 1

Introduction
Tell them about yourself and establish your credibility.
- Give brief background of this program (See Appendix A, Suggestions for Introductory Comments).

Review Purpose and Value of Program
Inform the volunteers that integrated into the training sessions will be model sessions. You will be demonstrating the session components and accompanying activities (warm-up, group focus, rhythm/ drumming, and closure).

Handout this Book and Do an Overview of the Chapters and Appendices

Question and Answer Period
- Discuss extra-curricular activities (hobbies, interests, clubs, etc.) they are currently doing.
- Talk about purpose of drum activities and what the benefits are. Older adults love to know why a certain activity is important.

Percussion/Rhythm Activities
Introduce the three sections of various activities. Spend some time talking about how to hold all of the drums and hand percussion instruments and demonstrate the various sounds that you can make with these instruments.

Warm-Up Activities
- *Egg Shakin' Blues*
- *Egg Shaker – Pass this Egg*

Group Focus Activities
- *Paddle Drum Ball Roll*
- *Steady Beat: Round and Round*

Rhythm/Drumming Activities
- *8-4-2-1 Rhythm Exercise*
- *Familiar Phrase Rhythm Training*

Discussion

Reflect on the activities. How do they feel? Talk about their energy change. Talk about their involvement. Could they see themselves doing this? Is this the kind of thing that they could do to teach others? Do you think that this would work in this center?

Confidentiality

We learn by doing, and we learn from and with each other. In order for all of us to feel safe and trusting, we ask that each of you observe a commitment of confidentiality about anything personal you hear during the training. That means you will not refer to anyone or anything you hear in these sessions in a way that could identify a member of the training group. Each trainee is unique and brings something special to the training group. We hope you will join with us in celebrating the uniqueness of each individual.

Have participants sign the "Consent for Use of Picture and/ or Voice" form before they leave (See Appendix A, Sample Consent Form Template).

Closure Activity

Choose familiar song(s)

Assignment

Have participants read the following sections:
- **INTRODUCTION** and **WORKING WITH OLDER ADULTS**
- **TRAINING CURRICULUM**; Responsibilities of Volunteers
- **TRAINING CURRICULUM**; Goals and Objectives of the Percussion/ Rhythm Program

Assign an activity from each of the aforementioned areas to the volunteers for next week. (EACH volunteer will lead ONE activity for next week.) Over the next three weeks, each volunteer should have an opportunity to lead all of the activities in each of the following areas: warm-up, group focus, drumming, and closure. By Week #4, they should have had experience in each of the session categories.

WEEK 2

Review Purpose and Value of Program

Review Percussion/Rhythm Activities (introduced in Week #1)
Introduce the three sections of various activities. Ask participants to
demonstrate how to hold all of the drums and hand percussion instruments and demonstrate the various sounds that can be made with these
instruments.

Warm-Up Activities
- *Egg Shakin' Blues*
- *Egg Shaker – Pass this Egg*

Group Focus Activities
- *Paddle Drum Ball Roll*
- *Steady Beat: Round and Round*

Rhythm/Drumming Activities
- *8-4-2-1 Rhythm Exercise*
- *Familiar Phrase Rhythm Training*

Review Reading Material (last week's assignment)

Introduce additional Percussion/Rhythm Activities:
Warm-Up Activities
- *Egg Shaker "Left-Right" Pass*
- *Rhythmic Names*
- *Three-Word Share*

Group Focus Activity
- *Group Patschen*

Rhythm/Drumming Activity
- *In-The-Moment Music*
- *Tandem Drumming*
- *Call and Response*

Closure Activity
Choose familiar song(s)

Assignment
Read through **TRAINING CURRICULUM**

WEEK 3

Review Purpose and Value of Program

Volunteers Facilitate all of the Following Percussion/Rhythm Activities

Introduce the three sections of various activities. Ask participants to demonstrate how to hold all of the drums and hand percussion instruments and demonstrate the various sounds that can be made with these instruments.

Warm-Up Activities
- *Egg Shakin' Blues*
- *Egg Shaker – Pass this Egg*
- *Egg Shaker "Left-Right" Pass*
- *Rhythmic Names*
- *Three-Word Share*

Group Focus Activities
- *Paddle Drum Ball Roll*
- *Steady Beat: Round and Round*
- *Group Patschen*

Rhythm/Drumming Activities
- *8-4-2-1 Rhythm Exercise*
- *Familiar Phrase Rhythm Training*
- *In-The-Moment Music*
- *Tandem Drumming*
- *Call and Response*

Review Reading Material (last week's assignment)

Feedback

It is important that the trainer give immediate feedback after the session is complete. If there are other participants in the group besides the volunteer trainees, dismiss those individuals before you give feedback. Even though it is all constructive, the volunteers will be more comfortable receiving the feedback amongst peer volunteers, and they will feel more comfortable discussing group issues.

Discussion

Talk about group dynamics. Talk about outreach possibilities in your community. Refer to Appendix B to discuss equipment recommendations. Let volunteers know that you will direct facilities (where volunteers will be working) to the appropriate vendors for purchasing necessary instruments.

Closure Activity

Choose familiar song(s)

Assignment

Have participants read the following: **ESTABLISHING OLDER ADULT VOLUNTEER PROGRAMS IN YOUR COMMUNITY** and **APPENDICES**

WEEK 4

Review Purpose and Value of Program

Volunteers Facilitate all of the Percussion/Rhythm Activities

See Week #3 – session plan

Give Feedback

Review Reading Material (last week's assignment)

Question & Answer Period

Make Assignments to Facilities Set Up By Trainer

Closure Activity

Choose familiar song(s)

As the trainer sets up programs for the volunteers, s/he will need to attend these sessions to mentor and support the volunteer facilitators. This helps them become more comfortable group leaders. You may need to do an orientation presentation at a facility in order to get an older adult volunteer established. Another suggestion is to invite potential facility administrators to your training program.

Tip: An example of a successful training program is the Resounding Joy, Inc. supportive music and recreational music-making program. If you are interested in learning more about this program, please go to their website - http://www.resoundingjoyinc.org.

MONTHLY SUPERVISION

Ongoing monthly supervision is a must. Choose a consistent day and time (e.g., every 4th Tuesday at 1:00 p.m.). These monthly meetings will continue to motivate and inspire volunteers. They can share new ideas and activities with their peers. If they are experiencing challenges, their volunteer peers and you can help to troubleshoot. The more experience they have in leading, the more confident they will be at their own facilities. Training increases motivation and shows the volunteers that they are important members of this program. Volunteers regard life-long learning as a very real benefit from their involvement in the program. Older volunteers like events where they can get together as a group, discuss their current duties, and learn new skills.

The trainer will need to use his/her best professional judgment in determining the appropriate amount of training for any one group.

45

DVD-TRACK 2*

EGG SHAKIN' BLUES – *Warm-Up*
By Gary Johnson, MT-BC

MATERIALS NEEDED
2 Egg Shakers for Each Participant
Song—"Egg Shakin' Blues" (next page)

OBJECTIVES
This activity is designed to help participants internalize a steady ostinato pattern while learning how to sing and play at the same time. This activity also serves as a good physical warm up for the hands and arms.

ACTIVITY DESCRIPTION
Participants begin playing shaker ostinato pattern. Leader begins singing the song encouraging others to join in. It is fun and helpful to model vocal improvisations during the "uh hu" breaks. All the movement words such as "up high" or "down low" should be accompanied by a movement. Other verses can and should be improvised by group members as they become comfortable with the song.

ADAPTATIONS
Seniors love to make up their own words with this song. For example:
I'm gonna shake in the attic,
I'm gonna shake in the cellar,
I'm gonna shake in the back porch, all day long.

46

*DVD-Track 1 is
an introduction
to the training
curriculum and
activities

> **Music Equipment**
>
> See Appendix B for details on percussion kits. The authors of this publication suggest **West Music Company, Inc.** for purchasing the recommended percussion kits. Please contact **West Music** at 1-800-397-9378 or email service@westmusic.com for more information.

ECC SHAKIN' BLUES – *Warm-Up* (Continued)

Egg Shakin' Blues ©

By Gary Johnson, MM, NMT, MT-BC

I'm gon-na shake, shake, shake— (un hu hu), I'm gon-na

shake, shake, shake----- (uh uh hu) I'm gon-na

shake, shake, shake— (uh uh hu) all day long I'm gon-na

1. shake, in the_ mor - nin',_ I'm gon-na shake in the_
2. shake up_____ high,_____ I'm gon-na shake down---------
3. shake to the_ right, -------------- I'm gon-na shake to the-

noon time,— I'm gon-na shake in the_ eve - nin'_
low, _____ I'm gon-na shake in the— mid - dle,_
left, _____ I'm gon-na shake all a - round me,—

all day long. I'm gon - na
all day long.
all day long.

* Take Liberties With Rhythm
* Repeat Chorus As Often As Desired

Printed by Permission of Gary Johnson, MM, NMT, MT-BC. May be reproduced and adapted without additional permissions. Please include composer credits in all reproductions in use.

47

EGG SHAKER "PASS THIS EGG" – *Warm-Up*
By Barry Bernstein, MT-BC

GROUP JUGGLES
Before beginning the activities below with the eggs, we recommend that you practice these exercises without the eggs until they have the rhythm and motion down and are able to verbalize the cues. Emphasize keeping the hand that receives the egg stationary and make big motions with the passing hand to fill the total time between passes.

TASK 1. ONE EGG PASS
Start with one egg in left hand. Teach the pass by giving the cues, "When I say the word 'AND,' reach over with your right hand to pick up the egg and when I say the word 'TAKE ONE,' take the egg, and when I say 'PASS ONE,' pass the egg to your neighbor's left hand" (egg is passed to the neighbor on your right). Then begin giving cues to a slow quarter note pulse. Encourage participants to say the cues out loud with you. As the group masters this, have them continue to pass their eggs while discontinuing the verbal cue.

TASK 2. "PASS THIS EGG" SONG
Teach group the song, "Pass This Egg" song. When they have learned the song, begin the pass as in Task 3; with the first pass occurring on the first "pass" in the lyrics of the song, continuing to pass the egg on every other quarter note throughout the song. Once the group has mastered this task, the group leader can begin to increase the tempo of the song.

Pass This Egg

Adapted from the song, *"The Shoe Game"*

I'm gon-na pass this egg from me to you, to you! I'm gon-na

pass   this   egg   so   do   just what   I   do!

48

EGG SHAKER "LEFT-RIGHT" PASS – *Warm-Up*
By Barry Bernstein, MT-BC

MATERIALS NEEDED
1 Egg Shaker for Each Participant

OBJECTIVES
This activity develops improved hand-eye coordination and an increased awareness of others.

ACTIVITY DESCRIPTION
This activity can be broken down to simple tasks so that each task can be mastered. It is recommended that you begin with Task 1 whenever using this activity for the first time with a group.

TASK 1. LEFT-RIGHT PASS
Start with one egg, which is held in the right hand. Begin singing "Left-Right Pass song, cuing participants to pass the egg from hand to hand with the song.

49

LEFT-RIGHT PASS

Barry Bernstein, MT-BC
Marcie Selvaggio, RMT-BC

	Left	right	left	right	left	right	left	right	left	right
OR	Pass	the	egg	from	one	hand	to	the	o-	ther.

TASK 2. LEFT-RIGHT PASS- with shake added on upbeat
Start with one egg, which is held in the right hand. Begin singing "Left-Right Pass" song but this time .... pass on the beat and shake the egg on the upbeat
L, shake, R, shake, L, shake, R, shake, L, shake, R, shake, L, R, L, R . . .

RHYTHMIC NAMES – *Warm-Up*
By Barry Bernstein, MT-BC

MATERIALS NEEDED
RhythmSticks
Drums/Mallets
Names of Participants

OBJECTIVES
This activity is designed to help participants hear and feel small rhythmical phrases.

ACTIVITY DESCRIPTION
Begin this activity by clapping familiar names. For example:

George   Wash - ing – ton

A - bra – ham   Linc – oln

John   F.   Ken- ne – dy

Say the name out loud in rhythm several times. Next, begin to say then clap the rhythm of the name as a call and response:

George Wash - ing - ton	*George Wash - ing - ton*
George Wash - ing - ton	*George Wash - ing - ton*
Su – san B. An - thon - y	*Su – san B. An - thon - y*
El - ean - or Roos - e - velt	*El - ean – or Roos - e – velt*

Experiment with clapping, and then progress to rhythm sticks and then to drums. Find the rhythm for each participant's name and have him or her lead the call and response.

ADAPTATIONS
1. Using participants' names, say and play each persons name in a 4/4 rhythm, four times. While one person plays a steady pulse on clave or bell, everyone plays his/her name at the same time. Build in a physical cue for hearing impaired persons.
2. Choose two names in the same meter and divide into two groups. Group 1 plays the first name while group 2 plays the second name. Begin by having them say the name, then say and play, then just play. After they can do this, have them exchange name rhythms in time (every 2 or 4 measures).
3. Cultural sensitivity is a consideration when working with multi-ethnic groups. Use political figures or other famous persons from cultures represented (e.g., Fidel Ramos, Carlos Salinas).
4. You can also use names of movie stars, fruits, vegetables, etc.

THREE-WORD SHARE - *Warm-Up*
By Barry Bernstein, MT-BC

MATERIALS NEEDED
Assorted Hand Drums and Hand Percussion

OBJECTIVES
This activity offers participants an opportunity to make individual choices within the group and encourages feelings of self-worth via the process of creative expression. It also provides an alternative means of social interaction and community building.

ACTIVITY DESCRIPTION
Have each group member choose an instrument he or she would like to play. Instructions are as follows: Go around the circle and ask individuals, one at a time, to say three words they feel lets the group know something about them. Have each group member say his or her name, state three words and conclude by playing a short improvisation on the chosen instrument.

Before beginning this group, the facilitator may want to model several responses in order to increase the comfort level of group participants. The facilitator may want to wait several sessions before trying this type of activity thus giving the group a chance to know each other better. Trying some of the adaptations prior to using this activity may also be helpful.

Once you have completed going around the circle ask everyone to repeat an improvisation similar to the one they had played a few minutes ago, but this time have everyone play their parts at the same time. Let this continue for as long as it feels comfortable for a beginning warm-up exercise.

ADAPTATIONS
To help make it less personal and threatening to the seniors, begin by using fill in the blank type activities.

"My name is Henry. I was born in Prairie Dog, Kansas."
"My name is Freda and I like to sail, or read, or watch TV . . ."

Any type of category can be used such as favorite Month, Season, Food, Car or Color.

PADDLE DRUM BALL ROLL – *Group Focus*
By Barry Bernstein, MT-BC

MATERIALS NEEDED
Paddle Drums
Nerf Balls (tennis ball size)

OBJECTIVES
This activity encourages increased hand-eye coordination and helps maintain fine motor control.

ACTIVITY DESCRIPTION
Give each participant one Paddle Drum and one Nerf Ball. Turn the drum upside down and place the ball inside the rim. Next, lead the group through a series of exercises, which encourage range of motion in the wrist.

1. Begin by pointing the drum up so that the ball rolls toward the handle and rests there. Now tilt the drum down so that the ball rolls straight across the drum to the opposite side. Repeat this several times.
2. Place the ball inside the rim as you did in #1. Tilt the drum to the right so that the ball rests against the rim in that position. Now tilt the drum to the left, rolling the ball across the drum to the opposite side. Repeat this several times.
3. Place the ball inside the rim as you did in #1. Tilt the drum in any direction, then begin a rolling motion so the ball rolls around the rim. Repeat this several times then change directions and roll the ball in the opposite direction.

When you have completed all three exercises switch hands and repeat #1-3.

GROUP PASS
This activity begins with one ball. Place the ball inside the drum as in #1. The object is to roll/pass the ball around the circle. When the group has mastered the pass, you can add more balls by staggering their introduction at the original entry point. See if you can get to the point where there are half as many balls as there are group members.

ADAPTATIONS
Place two balls in a drum and have participants pass the balls around the circle. Continue by adding 1-2 balls each additional round. Try up to 7-8 balls. You may want to play some flowing music in largo or adagio tempo as a background for this activity.

STEADYBEAT: ROUND AND ROUND – *Group Focus*
By Barry Bernstein, MT-BC

MATERIALS NEEDED
Paddle Drums/Hand Drums Assorted Hand Percussion

OBJECTIVES
This activity provides an opportunity for participants to develop a greater group awareness and encourages improved impulse control.

ACTIVITY DESCRIPTION
The first few times you use this activity try to use one type of instrument, i.e., use all Paddle Drums or Hand Drums. It is recommended that the hand percussion be used after the group has done this activity several times.

Sitting in a circle, count off, assigning each person a number. Begin counting all the numbers of the group (i.e., if there are 8 group members count from 1 to 8 repeatedly in a steady pulse manner). Instruct each participant to play their instrument only on their number. Try going around the circle in the steady pulse manner without counting out loud. You may try having one group member play a steady pulse on a clave or cowbell. This can provide some extra auditory cuing.

ADAPTATIONS
1. Experiment with getting faster/slower, or louder/softer.
2. Add a vocal sound to the percussion event. When it is your turn to play, say your name, say your favorite color or make some kind of vocal improvised sound.
3. Instead of using a steady quarter note pulse, participants can play any agreed upon 1-beat rhythm pattern when it is their turn.

CROUP PATSCHEN – *Group Focus*
By John Ivor Chester III

MATERIALS NEEDED
Group Sitting Close Enough to Touch Each Other's Knees

OBJECTIVES
Increase concentration. Increase gross motor movement.
Cross midline. Increase awareness of others—community building.

ACTIVITY DESCRIPTION
Using both hands, participants are instructed to do a four beat combination of knee pats involving both theirs as well as their neighbor's knees.

Beat 1. Pat your knees, left hand on left knee, right hand on right knee.

Beat 2. Pat your knees, crossing hands. Right hand on left knee, left hand on right knee.

Beat 3. Repeat Beat 1.

Beat 4. Pat both your neighbors' knees. Left hand on right knee of neighbor on your left, right hand on left knee of neighbor on your right.

Beat 4 requires some group reversal, as there is some crossing of each person's hands. Group members can work out who will go in or out. Try it and you will understand.

Once group has mastered the movements teach them the song, "Hida" (see song below), then perform the group patschen using the song as rhythmic structure. Experiment with getting faster and slower and singing louder and softer.

ADAPTATIONS
1. Sit and move feet to the above four-beat combination.
2. Use only hand movements for the four-beat combination.

YIDDISH FOLK SONG   *Traditonal*

HI-DA, HI-DA, HI-DIH-DEE-DI-DA, HI-DA,   HI-DA,HI-DA. HI-DA, HI-DIH-DEE-DI-DA,

HI-DA,   HI-DA, HI-DA,   HI-DA.   HI-DA, HI-DA.

8-4-2-1 RHYTHM EXERCISE – *Rhythm/Drumming*
By Barry Bernstein, MT-BC

MATERIALS NEEDED
Hands
Egg Shakers
Paddle Drums or Frame Drums

OBJECTIVES
Increase attention span & task orientation.
Encourage self-expression within structure.
Develop sense of pulse and rhythm skills.

ACTIVITY DESCRIPTION
Begin by having everyone in the circle play a steady ostinato, whether
it is a right-left knee pat, or a steady pulse egg shake, or on a paddle
drum/hand drum. When the group has entrained, without stopping,
demonstrate what eight measures of two beats feel like by counting
it out loud, 1/2/3/4/5/6/7/8/. (You can say, *"Eight feels like this ..."*)
While the group continues to play the ostinato, have each participant
play an eight-measure solo. Cue each person on the *"and"* of 8, *"and
Joe"* (Joe is used as beat 1). It is important to establish eye contact
with each person as you are giving him or her his or her cue to solo.
Continue around the circle several times.

Once this has been mastered, reduce the count to 4 then 2 and finally
1. Try each of these several times as was done above. Have the group
continue to play the pulse while you give the instructions for each new
section. Point out that each change cuts the time in half and that the so-
los will move around the circle twice as fast as in the previous segment.

ADAPTATIONS
1. Add a vocal sound or movement during your solo.

2. Other suggested body sounds that can be used are as follows: tap
knees or thighs, snap fingers, clap heels of hands, clap palms—
hands flat or curved, stamp, tongue clicks—forward (horse hoofs),
tongue clicks back (as in calling a dog), lip pops, blow out air, whisper,
moan, squeak, glide up and down, and make vowel sounds.

3. Using the 8 count, < crescendo starting with measure 1 (pp) to measure 8 (ff). Physical cues can be very effective as well as fun. Start with drum near floor and slowly raise drum as you get louder ending up with it above your head and returning to the floor for the next 1.

4. Play 4 or 8 counts of steady pulse followed by 4 or 8 counts of group improvisation. Go back and forth several times. Try adding dynamics (e.g., steady pulse—quiet; improvisation—loud). Alternate patterns with every other person, one group playing pulse while the other improvises. Alternate every 8 measures.

5. Rather than going around the circle, participants can establish eye contact with another member and "pass" the solo to that member when appropriate.

FAMILIAR PHRASE RHYTHM TRAINING – *Rhythm/Drumming*
By Barry Bernstein, MT-BC

MATERIALS NEEDED
Rhythm Sticks
Drums/Mallets
Hand Percussion Instruments
Poster Board & Stand

OBJECTIVES
This activity is designed to offer participants experience in feeling longer rhythmical phrases, as well as providing opportunity for improved social interaction.

ACTIVITY DESCRIPTION
Choose a familiar nursery rhyme, limerick or aphorism. Have the group say it out loud several times. Next, demonstrate how the rhythms of the phrase can be played on an instrument. Have the group say and play the phrase several times. When they feel comfortable with the rhythm, have them continue playing it without saying the phrase out loud. When using longer phrases such as limericks, it may be beneficial to write it out in large print on a poster board.

(Phrase 1):

Peas porridge hot,

Peas porridge cold,

Peas porridge in the pot,
Nine days old.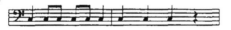

(Phrase 2) same rhythm:
Some like it hot, Some like it cold, Some like it in the pot,
Nine days old.

ADAPTATIONS
1. Divide the group into two smaller groups. Have Group I play phrase one, and Group 2 play phrase two. Then have them exchange parts in time every 1, 2 or 4 times.
2. Divide the group into two smaller groups. Have Group I play the entire phrase while Group 2 improvises over this pattern. Again, have them reverse in time.

FAMILIAR PHRASE RHYTHM TRAINING (Continued)

A bird in the hand
Is worth two in the bush.

An apple a day
Keeps the doctor away.

April showers bring May flowers.

A stitch in time saves nine.

Baa, Baa black sheep
Have you any wool?
Yes sir, yes sir
Three bags full.
One for my master
One for my dame
And one for the little girl
Who lives down the lane

Early to bed and early to rise
Makes a man healthy,
wealthy, and wise.

Good things come to those who wait.

Home is where the heart is.

Humpty Dumpty sat on a wall,
Humpty Dumpty had a great fall,
All the king's horses
and all the king's men
Couldn't put Humpty together again.

Jack and Jill went up the hill
To fetch a pail of water,
Jack fell down and broke his crown,
And Jill came tumbling after.

Jack be nimble, Jack be quick,
Jack jump over the candle stick.

Make new friends, but keep the old;
One is silver and the other's gold.

No Bees – No Honey.
No Work – No Money.

One, two, buckle your shoe;
Three, four, shut the door;
Five, six, pick up sticks;
Seven, eight, lay them straight;
Nine, ten, a big fat hen.

Peas porridge hot
Peas porridge cold
Peas porridge in the pot,
nine days old.
Some like it hot
Some like it cold
Some like it in the pot nine days old.

Rain, rain, go away
Come again another day.

IN-THE-MOMENT MUSIC – *Rhythm/Drumming*
By Barry Bernstein, MT-BC

MATERIALS NEEDED
Assorted Hand Percussion (e.g., claves, shakers, scrapers, cowbells, etc.)
Assorted Found Musical Instruments (e.g., kitchen utensils, etc.)

OBJECTIVES
This activity offers participants an opportunity to develop their listening skills while enhancing their group awareness. It also encourages improved self-image via the creative process.

ACTIVITY DESCRIPTION
Each person chooses a percussion instrument. It is best to not use drums for this activity as they do not offer a wide variety of timbres. The group facilitator begins with a set of claves, speaking about how the claves are the "time keepers" of the group. (In every set of claves, there is a "beater" and a "beatee.") The facilitator then begins playing the claves at whatever steady pulse feels comfortable. Each group member is encouraged to listen to the pulse and join in when they are ready. Before the activity begins, the facilitator can communicate about how satisfying it is to listen and find your spot in the rhythm. This should be demonstrated by playing some parts that fill up every part of the pulse, i.e., all 16th notes, and then playing some parts that only take up a small part of the pulse. The facilitator conducts the group, bringing in families of instruments (bells, woods, shakers, etc.) one at a time. He then cues individuals, directing attention to the total effect.

"Music Is Made of Sounds and Silences!"
—A metaphor for communication

Once the music has begun and everyone has joined in, let this first improvisation continue for a few minutes. You can end by counting eight beats backwards, 8/7/6/5/4/3/2/1/.

Give the verbal cue that you are going to count backwards from 8 to 1 and that the group should end on 1.

The activity continues by having everyone pass their instrument to the right (or left) and beginning to play again. The new clave player or

"time keeper" must choose a tempo to play their steady pulse. You may have to help them with the eight count cue to end.

ADAPTATIONS

1. When the facilitator feels the group would benefit from more structure they can use traditional conducting techniques to bring participants in and out of the improvisation. It may be useful to pass out instruments in groups (all the shakers sitting together, etc.).

TANDEM DRUMMING – *Rhythm/Drumming*
By Barry Bernstein, MT-BC

MATERIALS NEEDED
Paddle Drums with Mallets

OBJECTIVES
Increase social interaction.
Increase body awareness via crossing mid-line.

ACTIVITY DESCRIPTION
While sitting in a circle, have each person grip drum and point it toward the ceiling, then while continuing to grip the drum have them lay their hand thumb down on their knee so that the drum is parallel to the ground out in front of them. Everyone should be sitting close enough to play the drums of the neighbor on either side.

Begin by playing a slow steady pulse:

M (my drum), L (drum on left), R (drum on right)

The playing order is as follows: M, L, M, R, M, L, M, R, etc.

When getting started have the group say aloud:

"Mine, Left, Mine, Right", etc.

Always begin slowly to allow participants an opportunity to develop the movement circuitry in rhythm, then slowly increase the tempo.

ADAPTATIONS
Begin adding different rhythm figures either to the neighbor drums or to "My" drum. Try 8th notes, dotted 8th, 16th, or triplets.

61

CALL AND RESPONSE – *Rhythm/Drumming*

By Barry Bernstein, MT-BC

MATERIALS NEEDED
Rhythm Sticks
Paddle Drums with Mallets

OBJECTIVES
This activity is designed to develop participant's hand-eye coordination.

ACTIVITY DESCRIPTION
This activity begins by having the group leader sing a four-beat rhythm while modeling the playing technique by holding arms out in front as if playing a conga drum. As each rhythm is chanted, the participants are asked to echo the phrase first by singing it, then by singing and playing their "air" drum. There should be no rest between the time the leader plays and their response time. As participants become comfortable with this routine, begin to have them play rhythms with body sounds, such as clapping or knee patting. You may also stop having them sing the rhythm and begin to concentrate on just playing it.

The next step is to introduce the rhythm sticks, repeating the same procedure as described above. After several sessions, the drums may be introduced in the same manner.

62

ESTABLISHING OLDER ADULT VOLUNTEER PROGRAMS IN YOUR COMMUNITY

B y now you have an understanding of older adult characteristics and the percussion/rhythm curriculum and activities used in training volunteers to work with older adults. Now it is time to set up a program in your community. This section will provide you with the information needed to develop, market and conduct your own program to train volunteers in your community. We will take you through a step-by-step process to accomplish this.

MATERIALS

Many of the materials you will need to establish a program have been developed for you. These brief, to-the-point, and attractively presented materials can persuade people of your professionalism and foster their ability to remember the key points of your presentation. The materials that we suggest you purchase or develop are as follows:

- *"Group Rhythm and Drumming with Older Adults: Music Therapy Techniques and Multimedia Training Guide"*
- Percussion Instruments (See Appendix B, Equipment Recommendations)

We suggest that you develop your own business card and fact sheet regarding your specific program. If you need to develop your own written materials, first outline the important points then write the information concisely and clearly in an easy to-read format. Leave adequate margins, list facts and emphasize key points with headings. Remember, materials are used to communicate objective facts and ideas and to capture the attention of the reader. Therefore, be aware of the quality of the information, typing, printing and paper used. Well-written materials will make an immediate good impression.

Appendix B has suggested listings for basic 10-20 person percussion kits. We recommend that you talk to your music merchant about stocking the necessary kits. (Refer to Appendix C before approaching a music merchant in your community.)

STEPS TO SECURING SITES FOR TRAINING PROGRAM

Keep in mind that the volunteer training program is for older adults. The types of facilities that you may want to contact are senior nutrition sites, retirement communities, volunteer organizations, etc. (A detailed list can be found on pp. 69-70). We suggest that you take the following steps in securing a training site.

1. Call Decision Maker (usually the Administrator of a facility) to schedule an appointment to discuss the volunteer program.

    a. Go over the Fact Sheet (see Appendix A, pp. 93-94).

    b. Schedule a demonstration presentation. Follow suggestions for Week #1 of the training program.

    c. Leave literature.

2. Tell the Decision Maker that once volunteers are trained, their facility will have the potential of ongoing programming by a trained volunteer.

It is our experience that securing a site is relatively easy to do. Decision Makers usually want to implement a group percussion program at their site after the demonstration session. Administrators are constantly looking to add quality programming to their facility calendars. Usually after a Decision Maker has seen your work he or she wants to know what the investment is in staff time and facility resources and what the cost will be to them.

SECURING FINANCIAL SUPPORT FOR TRAINING PROGRAM

This will probably be a new program for many older adult sites. It is hoped and expected that you will be compensated to conduct these training programs and to do the follow-up and supervision of the volunteers as they begin to work in the community to ensure their success. Facilities may be able to afford your services in full or only in part. It is likely that you will need to find this financial support yourself. The following are suggestions for securing funds from both the public and private sectors:

"It is likely that you will need to find financial support yourself."

1. Do presentations for service organizations (e.g., Kiwanis, Rotary, Optimist organizations) to solicit funding for the training program. Emphasize how a minimal investment will benefit a wide spectrum of the community.

2. Approach several agencies—senior centers, Area Agencies on Aging (AAA), Chambers of Commerce, churches, etc.—to jointly fund the training program.

3. Look into grant programs sponsored by organizations such as community arts groups, state and local AAAs, local foundations and trusts, philanthropists, etc. If you need assistance in grant writing, contact AMTA or your local library for resources.

4. Have the volunteers individually pay a certain amount for the training. A sliding scale could be used to accommodate different income levels. Remember, when people make a monetary investment in training and materials, they will value it more and have more commitment to the process.

5. Hold fund-raising events such as a community drum circle. (You will likely want to work with an established group in your community such as a school, church or senior center.)

6. Work closely with a music store in your community. As a result of work with RBMT, relationships have been established in the music products industry. Based upon successful results of this joint effort, it is suggested that the private sector be approached when appropriate. Contact the International Music Products Association (http://www.namm.org) for assistance in identifying a music merchant in your area. (Refer to Appendix C for suggestions on how to approach individuals in the music products industry.)

Fees for your services will vary across the country. Remember, you should charge what is customary in your community.

FINDING VOLUNTEER TRAINEES

Now that you have a site and funding, you need volunteers for your training program. You will have interested persons just by demonstrating at the training site. However, developing a marketing plan is essential and should be completed as your first step. Marketing music therapy services involves developing a quality program, targeting potential consumers, and communicating effectively with those consumers. Thorough preparation can make the difference between success and failure (Henry, Knoll, & Reuer, 1999). Be aware that you need to be able to handle the outcome of a marketing program. It would be most embarrassing if you made public announcements and had the volunteers lined up but were not able to follow through with the training program. The following steps should be in your marketing plan. These will often happen simultaneously.

I. WRITE PRESS RELEASES

Place an announcement in your local paper about this program and that you are seeking volunteers (See Appendix A). Send a copy of your press release. Send your release to organizations and individuals with an interest in what you have to say. Select media recipients who are associated with media that focus on your target audience, particularly in terms of subject and geographical area. Regardless of whether you send the release to media or non-media contacts, take the time to find out the name and title of the appropriate contact. This will make the person more receptive to using the material. It also will facilitate your telephone and written follow-up. Tell them you will be doing a demonstration at XYZ senior center. Ask them to announce the need for volunteers.

Write releases so that the media is (1) able to prepare an article by copying all or part of the release, and (2) interested in contacting you for information for a more in-depth story. To generate coverage for an event, send the release enough ahead of time that a reporter and photographer can be detailed to cover it. Follow up two days before the event to encourage coverage. Facilitate media coverage. Prepare releases in ways that make it easy for the media to use your material:

> • *Meet deadlines.* Call the publication or media station to learn about deadlines that affect the timing of your news release, and send releases in time to meet deadlines.
> • *Make follow-up contact easy.* Include the name, title, telephone number, facsimile number, and address of a contact person at the top of the page.
> • *Double space the text.* Make it easy for the editor to mark your text for publication.
> • *Emulate the writing style of the type of publication targeted.* Make it easy for the editor to just insert your copy in available space. Press releases for academic journals, for example, should differ form press releases for the popular press. Write an effective lead. Produce a first paragraph that is brief, active, and conveys a new fact.

• *Use newspaper style.* Begin with the most important facts and end with the least important. Editors cut text from the bottom up.

• *Make it brief.* Write a one-page release, if possible. This is long enough to convey the message in most cases, and short enough to look inviting to an editor. An editor will call if more information is needed (Karsten & Kasab, 1990).

2. MAKE ANNOUNCEMENTS

Send an announcement to facilities such as the following regarding this training program (See Appendix A). The announcement should answer the questions: "Who, What, When, Where and Why?" You can go through your local yellow pages and find many of the names and addresses for the list below. Other resources are commercial publications (e.g., New Lifestyles, published in California which groups all aging facilities by county), the State Licensing Board for board and care homes, and the Area Agency on Aging. Facilities that can be contacted regarding the program are as follows:

• *Aging Network: AARP, Local Agency on Aging, County or City Council on Aging, etc.*
• *Arts Organizations*
• *Churches, Synagogues*
• *Community Colleges (Adult and summer education programs)*
• *Community Recreation Centers*
• *Community Service Centers*
• *Corporate Retiree or Pre-Retirement Programs*
• *Elderhostel Programs*
• *Foster Grandparents*
• *Health Clubs*
• *Learning Camps*
• *Libraries*
• *Multi-Ethnic Organizations*
• *Museums*
• *Musician's Union*
• *Music Stores*
• *Newspapers—Calendar section and volunteer section*
• *Retired Senior Volunteer Programs*
• *Retired Teachers Association Units*
• *Retirement Homes*
• *Schools (Send home announcements with children.)*

- *Senior Center Service Organizations (Meals on Wheels, Salvation Army, etc.)*
- *Senior Centers (Nutrition Sites)*
- *Senior Clubs (Check local papers)*
- *Singles Organizations*
- *Summer Day Camps*
- *Volunteer Bureau/Clearinghouse*
- *Volunteer Organizations*
- *YMCA/YWCA*

3. Place Public Service Announcements

Contact radio and television stations in your community and let them know that a program is starting in the community. To increase the likelihood of your public service announcement being aired especially at a radio station, prepare a 15-second and 20-second spot. Double space and type it in all caps.

4. Place Media Articles

Look for opportunities to place media articles. Prepare a short article about the group percussion/rhythm program and send to senior organizations, community service groups and allied health organizations to include in their newsletters. Write for your audience. Read several issues of the publication to which you plan to submit before beginning to write to get a feel for the style, tone, and length of articles similar in purpose to the one you will prepare. (When you place an article because of sending a release, order reprints or request written permission to reprint it yourself. Use the reprint to disseminate information about your project.)

5. Post Flyers, Brochures, and Business Cards

Post flyers, brochures, or business cards in key areas to increase public awareness of this new program. Community bulletin boards in churches, community recreation centers, senior citizen centers, music stores, and other high traffic areas (e.g., coffee shops, health clubs, book stores, libraries, etc.) are good possibilities free advertising. (Always ask permission to leave information to avoid any misunderstandings.) Information on these flyers should specify services offered, clientele, credentials, and contact information.

After you have done a mail campaign and posted flyers, etc., you should follow-up to schedule a presentation. Presenting prepared public awareness programs to various groups can be a good introduction to people concerned about wellness and health prevention issues of the older adult population.

CONDUCTING PROFESSIONAL PRESENTATIONS

A successful presentation requires careful planning—from determination of the areas of content, to the style used, to all the technical details. A detailed outline of your entire presentation including estimated time spans for each section of the presentation is an effective planning tool. A creative, non-threatening introductory activity may help stimulate interest. Rhythm-based music activities certainly assist the leader in defining the mood of a presentation. Get acquainted warm-up activities are included in this curriculum.

When presenting this group percussion/rhythm program, brief, understandable definitions of terms and concepts are generally more effective than lengthy book definitions. Communicating ideas clearly is the presenter's primary concern. To assure clarity, either avoid using jargon and define terms in advance and/or simultaneously with their use. To increase the usefulness of your personal contact, inform your audience about where and how to obtain and provide additional information. Always be prepared to distribute your business card (with name and telephone number of a contact person) when distributing a handout about the program (Karsten & Kasab, 1990).

PRACTICAL CONSIDERATIONS

Anticipating all emergencies such as faulty equipment and attending to details such as adequate supply of handouts can contribute to the success of a presentation. Arrangements for the provision of audio-visual aids and equipment should be made well in advance. All audio-visual aids should be previewed and equipment checked prior to presentation. Being familiar with basic equipment usage and maintenance procedures is extremely important if you deliver many presentations.

Physical facilities are an important consideration as well. The room should be large enough to accommodate the anticipated number of participants and equipped with a sufficient supply of chairs. A pleasant room temperature and adequate lighting will allow participants to concentrate on the program rather than their physical comfort. Allow as much pre-program preparation time as possible. Arriving early gives the presenter an opportunity to check room arrangements, equipment and other details without the pressure of time. Credibility must be earned. You demonstrate professionalism by dress, oral presentation and interaction with participants.

SPEAK EFFECTIVELY

Use tested techniques to help you create a good impression and get your point across. Wait until the end of the presentation to distribute brochures and/or handouts from a location close to the room exit (Karsten & Kasab, 1990). During the presentation, you need to begin punctually, stay on the topic and end on time. Conclude the session by restating the presentation's main points, rather than by leaving the audience to remember just the last few points.

"The wealth of our society is people and giving of their time."
—(Anonymous)

CONCLUDING REMARKS

This section has provided a brief overview of the how-tos in developing, marketing and conducting group percussion/rhythm programs. These are only guidelines; you will have to experiment to find what works in your community. Music therapists and others throughout the country have used the information provided in this training guide. They have found this information useful as a blueprint to follow.

BIOGRAPHIES

BARBARA REUER, PHD, MT-BC, NMT, is known internationally for her expertise in music-centered wellness and music therapy. Dr. Reuer, a graduate from the University of Iowa, is Founder and Director of MusicWorx of California, a contractual and consulting agency based in San Diego, CA. She has 30 years of clinical experience in public schools, convalescent facilities, retirement homes, hospices, medical and psychiatric hospitals, corrections facilities, substance abuse and eating disorders programs, health spas, and teaching at community colleges and universities. Major areas of Dr. Reuer's current professional involvement are in the area of music therapy program and job development in San Diego County including an international music therapy internship program. More recently, she has established *Resounding Joy, Inc.*, a non-profit organization to provide a supportive and healing music environment for adults and children who are homebound or have special needs.

In addition to clinical work, she provides workshops and seminars (wellness, community building, stress management) for healthcare professionals, educators and corporate clients. She has authored and co-authored several books and articles. Public notice of her work extends from recognition in publications to the Lifetime Network television show, *New Attitudes*. She has been interviewed in print media and television at the local, national and international levels.

Dr. Reuer has served as President of the National Association for Music Therapy (1996-97) and was the recipient of the Professional Practice Award from the American Music Therapy Association (2000) in recognition of significant contribution to the practice of music therapy. In 2006, she was awarded by her peers the Betty Isern Howery Award, at the Western Regional American Music Therapy Association conference, the highest award for professional contribution in the field of music therapy in the region.

BARBARA CROWE, MMT, MT-BC, is Professor and Director of Music Therapy at Arizona State University in Tempe, Arizona. She is a bridge builder and innovative thinker contributing to the profession of music therapy for nearly three decades as a clinician, author, educator, and leader. Her clinical experience stems from her work at the Neuropsychiatric Institute of the University of Michigan hospital working with emotionally disturbed adolescents and elsewhere with youth, adults and the elderly.

Professor Crowe has been very active in the American Music Therapy Association over the last twenty-five years, and its predecessor organization, the National Association for Music Therapy (NAMT). During her tenure as President of NAMT (1990-1991), she participated in a hearing before the United States Senate Special Committee on Aging entitled "Forever Young: Music and Aging," and contributed written testimony to the official hearing record. Barbara was awarded the Lifetime Achievement Award (2005) by the American Music Therapy Association.

Barbara served as Executive Director of the non-profit organization, Rhythm for Life. This unique organization promoted Rhythm-Based Music Therapy interventions and community drum circles for the elderly, at-risk youth, individuals in drug and alcohol treatment, and prison inmates. Professor Crowe coordinated, "Village Drumming," a community gang-prevention intervention for at-risk youth.

Professor Crowe's personal research agenda includes the historical antecedents of current Music Therapy practice and the newly emerging sound healing and subtle energy practices. Barbara is author of numerous publications including "Music and Soulmaking: Toward a New Theory of Music Therapy," "Implications of Technology in Music Therapy Practice," "Shamanism and Music Therapy: Ancient Healing Techniques in Modern Practice," and is Editor of "Best Practices in Music Therapy for Adults, Adolescents, and Children with Mental Disorders."

"BONGO" BARRY BERNSTEIN, MT-BC, is the creator and program director of the UNITY WITH A BEAT! programs. Sharing his wealth of knowledge about the educational and motivational power of rhythm, he has developed programs and presented papers on the benefits of music therapy for treating children with mental and physical disorders. With 25 years experience as a Music Therapist, workshop facilitator, and recording artist, Barry maintains an international schedule of providing services to schools, businesses, and healthcare facilities for his consulting company, HEALTHY SOUNDS. Currently he serves as the Music Therapy Consultant for the Blue Valley School District in Overland Park, KS.

BIBLIOGRAPHY

Alliance for Aging Research (AAR). (1996). Will you still treat me when I'm 65? Washington, DC.

American Medical Student Association (AMSA) - The senior boom is coming: Are primary care physicians ready? (2005). Retrieved April 20, 2005, from http://www.amsa.org/programs/gpit/seniors.cfm.

Bittman, B., Berk, L., Shannon, M., Muhammad, S., Westengard, J., Guegler, K. & Ruff, D. (2005). Recreational music-making modulates the human stress response: A preliminary individualized gene expression strategy. Med. Sci. Monit., 11(2): BR31-40.

Bittman, B., Bruhn, K., Lim, P., Neve, A., Stevens, C. & Knudsen, C. (2004, November). Focus on caregiving: Testing the power of music-making. Provider.

Butler, R.N., & Lewis, M.I. (1983). Aging and mental health. St. Louis, MO: C.V. Mosby.

Ciocon, J. A. & Potter, J.F. (1998). Age-related changes in human memory: Normal and abnormal.. Geriatrics, 43(10), 43-48.

Clair, A. (1996). Therapeutic uses of music with older adults. Baltimore, MD: Health Professions Press.

Clair, A. (2002). The effects of music therapy on engagement in family caregiver and care receiver couples with dementia. American journal of Alzheimer's disease and other dementias, 17, 5, 286-290.

Connor, B. (2002). Response guided errorless learning with normal elderly. Dissertation Abstracts International: Section B: The Sciences & Engineering, 62 (10-B), 4767.

Davis, W. B., Gfeller, K. E., & Thaut, M. H. (1999). An introduction to music therapy. Dubuque, IA: Wm. C. Brown.

Dychtwald, K. & Fowler, J. (1990). Age wave: The challenges and opportunities of an aging America. New York: Bantam Books.

GenAmerica – Aging facts. (2001). Retrieved April 25, 2005 from http://www.genamericaserve.com/agetalk/agingfacts.htm.

Henry, D., Knoll, C., & Reuer, B. (1999). *Music works: A handbook of job skills for music therapists*. Stephenville, TX: Music Works Publications.

Holmes, C., Knights, A., Dean, C., Hodkinson, S., & Hopkins, V. (2006). Keep music live: music and the alleviation of apathy in dementia subjects. *International Psychogeriatrics*, 18, 623-630.

Karsten, S. & Kasab, D. (1990). *Dissemination by design* (Award No. 90PD0129). Washington, DC: Administration on Aging, Department of Health and Human Services.

Kerin, R. A., Berkowitz, E. N., Hartley, S. W., & Rudelius, W. (2002). *Marketing*. McGraw-Hill/Irwin.

Leszcz, M. (1997). Integrated group psychotherapy for the treatment of depression in the elderly. *Group, 21(2)*, 89-113.

NCHS – Mortality data from the national vital statistics system. (2005). Retrieved April 20, 2005, from http://www.cdc.gov/nchs/about/major/dvs/mortdata.htm.

Peyser, M. (1999). *Home of the gray*. Newsweek, 133, 9, 50-53.

Prickett, C. A. (2000). *Music therapy for older people: Research comes of age across two decades*. In Effectiveness of music therapy procedures: Documentation of research and clinical practice (pp. 297-321). Silver Spring: American Music Therapy Association.

Raynor, T. (2007, Spring). *A banquet for hungry minds: Oasis nourishes the aging brain*. SUNY Upstate Medical University Outlook, 23-25.

Suzuki, A. I. (1998). The effects of music therapy on mood and congruent memory of elderly adults with depressive symptoms. *Music Therapy Perspectives*, 16, 75-80.

Suzuki, M., Kanamori, M., Watanabe, M., Nagasawa, S., Kojima, E., Ooshiro, H. & Nakahara, D. (2004). Behavioral and endocrinological evaluation of music therapy for elderly patients with dementia. *Nursing & health sciences, 6(1)*, 11-18.

Thaut, M. H., McIntosh, K. W., McIntosh, G. C., & Howmberg, V. (2001). Auditory rhythmicity enhances movement and speech motor control in patients with Parkinson's disease. *Functional neurology*, 16(2), 163-172.

U.S. Census Bureau – The 65 years and over population: 2000. (2001). Retrieved April 25, 2005 from http://www.census.gov/prod/2001pubs/c2kbr01-10.pdf.

U.S. Census Bureau - Census Bureau Frames U. S. in Global Context; Identifies Aging, Fertility Trends. (2002). Retrieved April 20, 2005 from http://www.census.gov/Press-Release/www/2002/cb02cn53.html.

U.S. Special Committee on Aging. (1990). *Hearing record forever young: Music and aging*. (DHHS Publication No. 102-9). Washington, DC: U.S. Government Printing.

Waters, E., Weaver, A., & White, B. (1980). *Gerontological counseling skills: A manual for training service providers* (2nd ed.). Rochester, MI: Oakland University Continuum Center for Adult Counseling and Leadership Training.

Welford, A. T. (1975). *Motivation, capacity, learning and age*. Paper presented at the 10th International Congress of Gerontology, Jerusalem, Israel.

Zedlewski, S. & Schaner, S. (2006, May). Perspectives on productive aging: Older adults engaged as volunteers. *Urban Institute, 5*, 1-7.

GLOSSARY

DRUM CIRCLE - A community event where a group leader or facilitator leads people in playing drums and hand percussion instruments.

DRUMMING - Playing drums (percussion instruments with stretched membrane heads) using hand, stick, or mallet.

ENTRAINMENT - The phenomenon whereby when two rhythms are nearly the same and their sources are in close proximity, their movement will fall into synchronicity.

FACILITATOR - An individual who serves as a group leader and who makes participation easy, pleasant and enjoyable for group members; one who assists the progress of the group.

GROUP PERCUSSION STRATEGIES - A series of carefully planned and selected percussion/drumming activities utilizing instruments, rhythmic patterns and techniques from a number of ethnic percussion traditions from around the world. Planning and selection of activities are driven by the participant population, their needs, abilities, and preferences.

INFIRMED OLDER ADULT - An older person whose physical, mental, emotional and/or social function is impaired by physical disease, emotional problems or severe social/economic factors.

INTERVENTION - A term used in therapy to denote an activity or approach used to remediate functioning problems or difficulties.

MUSIC THERAPY - is an established healthcare profession that uses music to address physical, emotional, cognitive, and social needs of individuals of all ages. Music therapy improves the quality of life for persons who are well, and meets the needs of children and adults with disabilities or illnesses. A music therapist is a trained professional who assesses client needs, plans and carries out music therapy interventions, evaluates, and participates in all aspects of the therapeutic effort.

PERCUSSION INSTRUMENT – An instrument such as a drum, xylophone, or maraca, in which sound is produced by one object striking another or by being scraped or shaken.

RBMT – Rhythm-based music therapy is a music therapy technique based on a client's active participation in a series of carefully selected and planned percussion/drumming activities. This technique uses instruments, rhythmic patterns and techniques from a number of ethnic traditions from around the world and emphasizes a cooperative, group-oriented model of participation.

VIBROTACTILE STIMULATION - Sensory stimulation created by physical vibrations of musical instruments and perceived by the sense of touch. Volunteerism - A person who performs a service or job of his/her own free will without pay.

WELLNESS MOVEMENT - The emphasis on disease prevention through healthy patterns of eating, exercise and stress management.

WELL OLDER ADULT - An adult person whose mental, physical and social functioning is within normal parameters for his/her age group—a person who does not have significant impairment in physical, cognitive, or social functioning

APPENDIX A
SUPPORT MATERIALS

SAMPLE CONSENT FORM TEMPLATE*
(USE YOUR FACILITY OR PRIVATE PRACTICE LETTERHEAD)

I hereby authorize *(insert organization name)* to use the images, voice, words and photographs of my child/dependent/self, and/or copies of these recordings or photographs in any editorial, publication, training material, promotional material produced and/or published by *(organization name)*, hereinafter collectively referred to as "digital resources."

I hereby release and hold harmless *(organization name),* the advisory board, board of trustees, officers, administrators, employees, and staff from including but not limited to retail sales of the digital resources, in whatever form and through whatever media.

I agree to make no claim for compensation for the uses of my image, voice, words and photograph of my child/dependent/self in the editorial, production, distribution, marketing, and/or other activities related to the digital resources. I hereby cede all rights, title, and interest in the digital resources to which I may be entitled by law to *(organization name)*.

I understand that signing this release does not guarantee public use of the digital resources. I waive any right I may have to inspect or approve the finished product or the advertising or other copy that may be used in connection therewith or the use to which it may be applied.

In executing this release, I certify that I am eighteen years or older.

91

_____

Participant   Date

_____

Witness or Legal Guardian (if necessary)   Date

_____

Music Therapist and/or Volunteer   Date

*Suggested template. Your legal counsel or that of partner agencies should address legal and/or regulatory questions. In addition, volunteers may be asked to sign a Business Associate agreement if the Older Adult Facility is a covered entity under HIPAA.

SUGGESTIONS FOR INTRODUCTORY COMMENTS

Brief Background of the Program

The United States and the entire world are currently experiencing a demographic revolution. In a little over 200 years, life expectancy in the United States has doubled. For the first time in history, a society of healthy active older adults has emerged. Throughout recorded history only 1 in 10 people could expect to live to the age of 65. Today nearly, 80% of all Americans will live past that age.

Until recently, work dominated the waking hours, and most men and women worked right up until the died. That has now changed. What is happening in America is happening in both developed and developing countries all around the world. There have been baby booms before but never a senior boom. Living a healthy, active life style has become of major importance to older Americans. More and more of them have taken care of their bodies and are concerned about physical fitness. Wellness and enrichment of life are the objectives of many older Americans.

While documentation shows that many music therapy strategies have been effective with the infirmed elderly, little formal use of specific music therapy techniques and strategies have been noted for well older adults.

To address this situation, individuals from San Diego State University Center on Aging in cooperation with the Rhythm For Life™ Project and the National Association for Music Therapy* conducted a one-year project funded by the Administration on Aging which was completed in December 1994. Though music therapy practices utilize a wide variety of music activities, group percussion strategies were chosen because research indicates great potential for the use of these activities with well older adults, and because rhythm is the basis of all music, and in fact, all life. Involvement in the rhythmic aspects of music is basic and primal. Research indicated that group percussion/rhythm experiences for older adults had the potential to offer a number of benefits such as immediate reduction of feelings of loneliness and nonverbal communications. The natural results of participation were increased self-esteem, enhanced ability to focus the mind, and group percussion/rhythm experiences were just plain fun.

*In 1998, NAMT became the American Music Therapy Association (AMTA).

FACT SHEET: VOLUNTEER TRAINING PROGRAM

Drumming for Health and Wellness (or title you choose)

Purpose

To train well older adult volunteers to conduct recreational, diversional group percussion activities for the following reasons:

1. Motivating: Response to rhythm is basic to human functioning making these percussion activities and techniques highly motivating in people of all ages and backgrounds.

2. Broad Appeal: Pure percussion activities are interesting and enjoyable to all people regardless of ethnic and cultural background, musical preferences or age range making these activities useful in creating groups that are fun and positive for a wide variety of people.

3. Physical Benefits: Participation in active group percussion experiences has physical benefits including sustained activity and use of fine motor skills.

4. Social Aspects: A strong sense of group identity and a feeling of belonging is created because: (a) participants are actively making music together and (b) the sustained repetition of the steady beat acts to bring people together physically, emotionally and mentally. The natural results are increased self-esteem, an enhanced ability to focus the mind and a rewarding social outlet.

5. No Musical Training Necessary: Percussion activities can be done with little or no previous musical background or training, making these experiences available to people from any socioeconomic level and easy for senior volunteers to learn and teach to others.

6. Multi-Ethnic: These techniques use multi-ethnic instruments and activities, which are increasingly important in our multi-ethnic society.

Cost

The consultation fee for this 4-week program is $x. (You will charge what is customary in your community.) For this, you will receive:

1. 4 three-hour group sessions,

2. Volunteers trained during the 4 weeks to keep the program going (at no cost) after the completion of the training,

3. The use of the equipment throughout the 4 weeks with the option to purchase the equipment at the end of the training, and

4. A mentor program, which will provide follow-up to your volunteers in order to maintain enthusiasm with new techniques and strategies.

Equipment

Equipment will be provided by a music store or yourself, free of charge throughout the training program. The facility can make arrangements with a music merchant recommended by you. Refer to Appendix B when discussing the equipment needs.*

* The authors of this publication suggest **West Music Company, Inc**. for purchasing the recommended percussion kits. Please contact **West Music** at 1-800-397-9378 or email service@westmusic.com for more information.

SAMPLE PRESS RELEASES

Possible Headings:

Drumming: More Than a Beat!
Music Project to Start with an Upbeat Note
Seeking Older Adult Volunteers Aging in Style . . . We are Doing It
Drumming for Health and Wellness

---

1. **"Program Name** *(Be Creative)***":** A program, which introduces recreational percussion activities for senior adults. Participants will experience the energizing effect of rhythm through drum circles, movement and percussion activities in a social setting. No musical experience necessary; class is for beginners as well as music enthusiasts. 4weeks, $x plus materials.

Wednesday

9/25/08 – 10/16/08

9:30-12:00 a.m.

Open to seniors

---

2. Volunteers Sought: ***Resounding Joy, Inc.***™* is seeking volunteers for a 4-week volunteer training (Joy Giver) program. Mary Bell, music therapist, will teach senior citizen volunteers basic percussion techniques and instruments. Seniors do not need a music or percussion background to participate. An informational meeting begins at 10:00 a.m. July 1 at the Senior Center. Call Bell at 123-4567.

---

*Note: Secure permission from **Resounding Joy, Inc.** (htty://www.resoundingjoyinc.org) before issuing a press release using **Resounding Joy** name.*

APPENDIX B
EQUIPMENT RECOMMENDATIONS

EQUIPMENT RECOMMENDATIONS

These kits have been put together by the authors with several factors in mind including sound quality, durability and ease of transport. Many other instruments can be used in this type of program. These kits are the basic instruments needed in a systematic rhythm-based program. Depending on your skill level and the skill level of your participants, many other drums such as congas, djun-juns, djembes and talking drums can be added to your instrument collection.*

10 Person Percussion Kit		**10-20 Person Percussion Kit**	
Qty.	Item	Qty.	Item
4	10" Paddle Drums	5	10" Paddle Drums
4	12" Paddle Drums	5	12" Paddle Drums
20	Egg Shakers	20	Egg Shakers
1	Small Djembe	2	12" Hand/Buffalo Drums
1	Small Doumbek	1 set	Shape Drums
1	Tambourine	1	Small Djembe
		1	Small Doumbek
		2	Tambourine
		1	Tubano

Other home-made or purchased percussion instruments (maracas, claves, cabasas, woodblocks, etc.) can be added as needed.

Note: These instruments are easily stored and transported in rolling carts that can be purchased at local office supply stores.

* The authors of this publication suggest **West Music Company, Inc**. for purchasing the recommended percussion kits. Please contact **West Music** at 1-800-397-9378 or email service@westmusic.com for more information.

DRUMS ... a few examples

Because of their depth, the BUFFALO DRUMS have a great sound – much more resonant than a hand drum. They are often associated with the sounds of tribal indigenous and Indian music.

DJEMBE is the traditional "long distance phone" of West Africa. Presently the djembe is the most popular African drum played in Europe. The drums have a wide tonal range with crystal clear heights and a rich deep bass sound, and have replaceable heads.

The DOUMBEK originates from the Middle East and Turkey. Traditionally played on the lap, the doumbek gets its name from its two basic sounds: The open bass (dum) sound, and a sharp, closed (bek) sound.

PADDLE DRUMS can be played anywhere. They are an innovation of Remo, Inc. They are wonderful to use in drum circles or anywhere because of their portability and great sounds. Paddle drums come individually in six sizes, or in three different sets offering choices of drum sizes and sounds.

The SOUND SHAPE drums are fun for groups of any size. Pre-tuned drum heads create a colorful, lightweight, incredibly portable instrument.

The TUBANO has a conga-like sound. It features an internal resonating tube and four molded feet to allow full resonance without using a floor stand or tilting the drum.

ZERO BUDGET INSTRUMENTATION
By Margery Baumgartner, Older Adult Volunteer

A quality musical experience requires good instruments. However, you may need to adapt instruments until you are able to purchase a full line of instrumentation for your group percussion/rhythm program. The following are suggestions on how to take items from home and convert them into musical, rhythmical instruments:

Bamboo Brush - Roll heavy paper or news and fringe end

Bells - Jingle bells attached to elastic wristband

Castanets - Walnut shells with tape finger loops; buttons with hat elastic through holes tied at bottom

Chopsticks - Half coconut shells, sandpaper mounted on blocks (rub)

Cymbal - Pot lids, tap with fingernails, thimbles, acorn hats

Drums - Gallon milk jugs, base of oatmeal box, can, bowl, wastebasket; head of leather, inner tube; sides with fabric (glued); mallets of chopsticks, wooden spoons, lengths of broomstick, top with padded sock, wooden bead, rubber super ball

Gong - Pot lid (strike against table)

Rainstick - Long or short cardboard tube stuck with pins or nails, filled with   sand or rice, ends closed; invert slowly

Rattles - Keys on string; small milk cartons and cans (soda, band aid, baking powder) filled with sand, rice, lentils, popping corn

Scrapers & Rasps - Washboard, grater, oven grate, pancake turner, masher, notched stick

Stretch rubber bands across tissue box (elevate with pencils)

Tambourine - Pie pan hung with bottle caps, buttons, washers, shells

Tape Bottles or Glasses - Tune with varying amounts of water

APPENDIX C
STRATEGIC ALLIANCES

STRATEGIC ALLIANCES: THE MUSIC PRODUCTS INDUSTRY AND THE MUSIC THERAPY PROFESSION AN IDEA WHOSE TIME HAS COME

We have included the following information as a resource. It can be used in several ways:

1. Parts of it can be copied as a handout for the music merchant.
2. You can refer to this material when you are preparing for your presentation to the merchant.
3. In addition to the demographic and marketing information, we have also provided an abbreviated plan of action for you to follow when you make your introduction to the music merchant.

A DEMOGRAPHIC REVOLUTION

The United States and the entire world are currently experiencing a demographic revolution. In a little over 200 years, life expectancy in the United States has doubled, and according to the National Center for Health Statistic, life expectancy continues to rise (NCHS, 2005). For the first time in history, a society of healthy, active older adults has emerged. Throughout recorded history, only one-in-ten people could expect to live to the age of 65. Today nearly 80% of all Americans will live past that age. Experts claim that by the year 2050, the average life expectancy of men and women in the U.S. could reach 89, up from 76 in 1995 (Peyser, 1999). This increase leads to a dramatic rise in the oldest segment of our population; Americans 85 and older are the fastest growing segment of the U.S. population (American Medical Student Association, 2005). In 1996, there were almost 4 million people in the U.S. over 85 years old. By the year 2040, 13 million Americans will be older than 85 (Alliance for Aging Research, 1996), an increase of more than thirty fold (U.S. Census Bureau, 2002). Until recently, work dominated the waking hours and most people worked right up until they died. That has changed. There have been baby booms before, but never a senior boom (Dychtwald & Fowler, 1990). The over-65 population in the United States will soon number 40-45 million representing one-fifth of the population. The older adult population will increase dramatically (both in numbers and as a percentage) during the first part of the 21st century.

MUSIC THERAPY PRACTICE

Music therapy practice with infirmed or frail elderly people in nursing homes and adult daycare settings is extensive and well documented (Prickett, 2000). A variety of music therapy activity interventions including group singing, reminiscing activities and movement to music are used to remediate a variety of problem areas (Davis, Gfeller, & Thaut, 1999). Recent research has shown that music therapy activity interventions are effective in promoting improved walking gait in stroke patients, improved movement and speech in patients with Parkinson's disease (Thaut, et al., 2001), decreased depression (Suzuki, 1998), improved social and interpersonal interactions (Clair, 2002) and improved cognitive functioning of persons with Alzheimer's disease (Suzuki, et al., 2004). Music therapists are well aware of the benefits of music therapy interventions with infirmed elderly clients. Recent studies are supporting the need for more evidence-based proactive protocols for recreation music-making as a means of inspiring creativity and wellness amongst older adults (2006; Bittman, Berk, Shaman, et al., 2005; Bittman, Bruhn, Lim, et al., 2004).

THE WELLNESS MOVEMENT

Living a healthy, active life style has become of major importance to all Americans. More and more of us are concerned about physical fitness. Wellness and enrichment of life are the objectives of many Americans. This is especially true of older people.

The customary ways of dealing with the aged population in the United States (institutional housing and costly, reactive medical interventions) will no longer be viable because of the enormous costs and the changing needs of a much larger and more active senior population. Several needs arise from this situation including:

1. Specific training and models of involvement and volunteerism that encourage and promote useful contributions to society for active well older Americans; and

2. The need for community-based programs and opportunities to promote communication between generations and prepare citizens for the aging process.

RHYTHM-BASED MUSIC THERAPY

Rhythm-based music therapy (RBMT) is a music therapy technique based on client's active participation in a series of carefully selected and planned percussion/drumming activities. This technique uses instruments, rhythmic patterns and techniques from a number of ethnic traditions from around the world and emphasizes a cooperative, group-oriented model of participation. RBMT techniques were selected as a basis for this program to train volunteers to conduct recreational, diverse group percussion activities for the following reasons:

> • Response to rhythm is basic to human functioning making these RBMT percussion activities and techniques highly motivating;
> • Pure percussion activities are interesting and enjoyable to all people regardless of ethnic and cultural background, musical preferences or age range making these activities useful in creating groups that are fun and positive for a wide variety of people;
> • Participation in active group percussion experiences has physical benefits including sustained physical activity and use of fine motor skills;
> • A strong sense of group identity and a feeling of belonging is created because: (a) participants are actively making music together; and (b) the sustained repetition of the steady beat acts to bring people together physically, emotionally and mentally (a process known as rhythmic entrainment);
> • Percussion activities can be done with little or no previous musical background or training making these experiences accessible to people of all socioeconomic levels thus making it easy for senior volunteers to learn and teach each to others; and
> • These techniques use multi-ethnic instruments and activities, which are increasingly important in our multi-ethnic and diverse society.

107

EXPANDING MUSIC PRODUCTS MARKET TO THE OLDER POPULATION

The 60 million Americans over age 50 are turning out to be the most powerful consumer group in history. Although they (currently) represent only about 20% of the total U.S. population, they control over 70%

of the net worth of U.S. households (Kerin, et al., 2002). Expanding the music products market to these individuals should be considered an opportunity. There will always be a youth market, but it will not always be as powerful relative to other markets. Older adults have specific market needs.

- Mature consumers need to be approached as active, interested consumers.
- Mature customers are interested in purchasing experiences more than just things. Convenience and access may be just as important as the product and service itself. Security and safety are important.
- They show a strong commitment to spending on products and services that enrich their lives (Dychtwald & Fowler, 1990).

Throughout history most social phenomenon have repeated over and over again. However, we have never before had such a massive population of middle-aged and older men and women. It is no wonder that we do not yet know how to effectively reach and serve this market. We must think of it as an opportunity.

MUSIC PRODUCTS INDUSTRY AND MUSIC THERAPY PROFESSION

Neither the music products industry nor the music therapy profession has taken sufficient advantage of the resources each has to offer the other in promoting the benefits of music and music making. However, because of this RBMT program, partnerships between the music therapy profession and the music products industry have developed. Leaders should explore this alliance in their plans to offer group percussion/rhythm programs in their communities. If you are interested in working with a music merchant, contact the International Music Products Association (http://www.namm.org) for assistance in identifying a music merchant in your area. Once you have identified the music merchant, consider the following points before approaching that merchant:

1. Many people in the music products industry have turned their love of music into a profession. The main thing to remember is that the music products industry is largely made up of individual

who know and understand the power of music and the importance of music education at an early age. While they may not be familiar with music therapy specifically, these individuals should be recognized as potential supporters and allies.

2. The music products industry is always looking for new markets to serve. The group percussion/rhythm program is just such a market. Traditionally, the music products industry has looked to the youth market for a high number of its sales. The group percussion/rhythm program for older persons and the wellness movement offer new marketing opportunities for the music products industry.

3. The music products industry has learned that it is essential for new programs to succeed quickly. Even good programs can fail, usually for the wrong reasons. For example, lack of resources (people, money and equipment) or negative word-of-mouth can virtually kill a program. This may create skepticism. To avoid such problems, carefully plan your approach to a music merchant before beginning your program.

109

LET US MAKE A FEW ASSUMPTIONS

Many, maybe even all, of the leaders who would like to offer the group percussion/rhythm program in their communities simply do not own or have access to the necessary equipment to offer the program—even to conduct sample programs. If it were necessary for them to purchase equipment in order to launch the program, it most likely would create somewhat of a financial burden. Entering into a partnership with a local music merchant is one way to deal with this problem.

HOW CAN AN ALLIANCE WITH A MUSIC MERCHANT IN YOUR AREA HELP?

A well-established music merchant may, for example, have excellent contacts in the area and may be able to arrange favorable introductions for the leaders to meet and discuss the program and offer sample demonstrations in appropriate settings. The music merchant may be willing to supply the necessary musical equipment at no charge for the sample demonstrations. In addition, because favorable exposure is always desirable, a music merchant may support the program in other ways. Because of the excellent support that this program received from the music products industry, we are providing an action plan in approaching the music merchants.

When approaching a music merchant, leaders should proceed as follows:

1. Make a list of candidates (prospects) for the program. The list should be prepared by category (e.g., senior nutrition sites, retirement communities, etc.). The list of potential organizations and locations should be exhaustive and well researched. It is important to determine the potential for the program. Refer to Chapter IV for other site suggestions and marketing tips.

2. Prepare to make a presentation to a music merchant. Call the music merchant and tell him/ her that you would like to meet to discuss a business opportunity and explain that you will need about an hour. Prepare your presentation. Approach the music merchant with a program not for a program. Follow guidelines in Chapter IV in preparing your presentation.

3. Gather materials for the presentation:
   • Materials from this Appendix
   • AMTA literature: *"Music Therapy and the Music Products Industry"*

4. When you meet the music merchant, you will explain that you are offering a business opportunity, really a partnership arrangement, and provide the necessary background information. Tell the music merchant that you plan to offer the program in the area, targeting decision makers in the Aging Community. Explain that you would like to develop a partnership based on the following:
   • You (the leader) would like to offer the 4-week pilot program in the area.
   • The program requires some percussion equipment (packaged for easy transportation) and other support.
   • Emphasize that the program offers potential sales and public relations for the music merchant.

5. It can be assumed that a number of community organizations will try the program and will elect to continue it with the trained volunteers. Volunteer leaders may want to learn new additional techniques and strategies. Work with music merchants on finding

financial support for on-going training workshops. The merchant and the therapist can work together to offer event drum circles quarterly or biannually. "Celebrities" (local or national) can be invited to participate. A fee could be charged. Promotion will be necessary. Public relations opportunities are excellent.

Partnerships between music merchants and leaders are an idea whose time has come. The opportunity exists now! This alliance will benefit everyone—merchants, music therapists, music leaders, activity directors, older adults, and the community.

APPENDIX D
DIGITAL VIDEO DISK CONTENTS

DIGITAL VIDEO DISK CONTENTS:
GROUP RHYTHM AND DRUMMING TECHNIQUES
AND DEMONSTRATIONS